*Rites of Privacy a*

# Rites of Privacy and the Privacy Trade

*On the Limits of Protection for the Self*

ELIZABETH NEILL

McGill-Queen's University Press
Montreal & Kingston · London · Ithaca

© McGill-Queen's University Press 2001
ISBN 0-7735-2097-X (cloth)
ISBN 0-7735-2113-5 (paper)

Legal deposit first quarter 2001
Bibliothèque nationale du Québec

Printed in Canada on acid-free paper

This book has been published with the help of a
grant from the Humanities and Social Sciences
Federation of Canada, using funds provided by the
Social Sciences and Humanities Research Council of
Canada.

McGill-Queen's University Press acknowledges the
financial support of the Government of Canada
through the Book Publishing Industry Development
Program (BPIDP) for its activities. It also acknowledges the support of the Canada Council for the Arts
for its publishing program.

Excerpts from *Essays on Moral Development*, Vol. 2.
*The Psychology of Moral Development* by Laurence
Kohlberg, copyright © 1984 by Laurence Kohlberg.
Reprinted by permission of HarperCollins
Publishers, Inc.

---

**Canadian Cataloguing in Publication Data**

Neill, Elizabeth, 1962–
    Rites of privacy and the privacy trade: on the limits
    of protection for the self
    Includes bibliographical references and index.
    ISBN 0-7735-2097-X (bound)
    ISBN 0-7735-2113-5 (pbk.)
    1. Privacy, Right of. I. Title
    JC596.N45 2001      323.44'8'01      C00-900613-3

---

This book was typeset by Typo Litho Composition
Inc. in 10.5/13 Palatino.

*With love to my late father,*
*Sam D. Neill,*
*who believed in this new millennium, and in me.*

# Contents

# Diagrams

# Acknowledgments

I wish to acknowledge the helpful assistance of Barry Hoffmaster, Richard Bronaugh, and Samantha Brennan, who provided useful commentary and suggestions on the earliest drafts of the manuscript. Sue Campbell, Alison Wylie, and, (once again) Samantha Brennan aided with further advice and commentary towards the development of this work into its present form.

I received assistance with computer glitches from several people at the "Help Desk" in the University of Western Ontario's Computer Science department; Jonathan Lindemann was particularly helpful. Marianne Welch of Western's law library spent minutes producing cases it would have taken me hours to find on my own.

I wish to thank the editorial staff at McGill-Queen's University Press, in particular Joan McGilvray, for cheerful responses to inane questions, and Claire Gigantes, my copy editor, for cleaning up after me. Thanks to Ron Schoeffel for warm encouragement.

On a personal note, I wish to thank my mother, Mary Neill, for proofreading, companionship, and good lunches. My sons, Shannon, Sandor, and Liam, provide laughter, love, and the best reason to take a break every day. Rob provides all that and anything else that matters.

*Rites of Privacy and the Privacy Trade*

# Introduction

Twentieth-century literature on the human right to privacy is striking, both because of the range of the theoretical opposition regarding the value and status of this "right," and because periodical literature of the last decade has largely abandoned theoretical considerations in favour of pragmatic ones. By this I mean that most current literature assumes a right to privacy, at least insofar as such a right has been bestowed through entrenchment in constitutions and legislation, and focuses on resolving specific issues in the fulfilment of this right for determinate individuals and groups. In other words, questions about the existence of this right, such as "Do we have a right to privacy and, if so, is it an innate human right or one born of cultural ideology?" have evolved into questions about its extent, for example, "How much privacy is too much privacy?" Definitional, or "what," questions regarding just what it means to possess a right to privacy have become fulfilment, or "how," questions regarding what it will take to give people a sense that their privacy is being protected.

It is hard to see that those earlier questions regarding the fact and nature of our right to privacy have been in any way resolved at the theoretical level. Democratic laws and constitutions are often put in place in response to the desires of majorities – and sometimes minorities – who create irresistible political climates but whose desires sometimes do not warrant fulfilment according to the underlying cultural ideology of entitlement. That analysis of cultural beliefs about the right to privacy has been largely abandoned may well stem from the fact that the demand for privacy, in the wake of burgeoning information and computer technologies, has become too great and outstripped the pace at which theory evolves. Societies, however, like individuals, can easily find themselves trapped by local politically determined measures of expediency, which are intended to meet the specific demands of specific individuals and groups but which ultimately clash with more global cultural beliefs. The fundamental motivation of this book, then, is to engage with the still-unstable theoretical basis of the rampant bestowal of a right to privacy in the current technological age. While much has been written about the need for such a right in such an age, little has been done to address the "whether" and the "what" of it in a way that seeks both to understand the emergence of theoretical discrepancies regarding privacy and to explain such discrepancies through a coherent theory of what it is in the nature of our beliefs about entitlement that lends our right to privacy so many faces. A clear delineation of these issues has the potential to check the unwarranted proliferation of the right and to ensure its security where it is legitimate.

There are those who define our right to privacy very narrowly, as constituting the right to control the possession and disclosure of specific facts about one's self, and those who define it very broadly and simply, as the right "to be let alone." I take the position that any attempt at definitional encapsulation in any but the most metaphorical sense is misguided because in a definitional or descriptive sense, our right to privacy is structurally complex. The failure of those who have attempted to produce more complete theories of privacy to recognize the nature of this structural complexity has given rise to vast theoretical oppositions. Reductionist views that see privacy as definable in terms of negative freedom[1] or privacy rights as reducible to other legal and moral rights, such as those we hold over property and person,[2] stand in stark opposition to theories that see our right to privacy as distinct and as something we have in virtue of inherent human dignity.[3] By the same token, communitarian theories of rights that see an interest in privacy as an emergent element of materially and socially advanced cultures alone[4] stand opposed to natural rights theories that see privacy and other rights as rights with which we are born as members of a moral community, and as bearers of human dignity.[5]

In both extreme positions the pivotal philosophical question is that of the ontological status of human dignity in relation to privacy, and, on the basis of that status, of the legitimacy of any privacy rights said to be grounded in it. Each of the four theoretical positions I have mentioned presupposes a particular stance regarding human moral personhood, notably with respect to whether and for what reasons it requires or does not require protection for and control over its innermost "sacred" self.[6] While it cannot be debated that society does (indeed, all societies do) provide a degree of protection for the privacy of the individual as well as for the conception of personal privacy as connected to human dignity, theorists continue to dispute both the source of this right – whether it is innate or a product of culture – and the degree to which it may supersede the interests of society.

As noted above, discrepancies in the literature on privacy cannot be resolved without first establishing a clear theory of our ideology of entitlement; for that ideology underlies the existence of our right to privacy, and the complexity of the ideology underlies our confusion about that right. An "ideology of entitlement" is, as I understand it, a culturally developed and sanctioned theory of rights. It comprises those beliefs to which we appeal in legitimating rights claims and that will be seen to be developed, by cultures, on the basis of innate human properties. While my sympathies lie with those who see privacy itself as linked to human dignity and privacy rights as staked *upon* human dignity, the literature lacks a description of the nature of human dignity that can adequately demonstrate dignity's power to produce rights. In particular, the ontological status of human dignity, whether it is an innate human quality or a societally bestowed quality, has not been determined. Given our tendency to view natural entitlement as more absolute than bestowed entitlement, determining the ontological status of human dignity is critical to a theory of rights. Just how does dignity inhere in people?

Thus, in order to resolve theoretical conflicts regarding our right to privacy, I shall depict the moral world of entitlement by describing the structure of rights in a way that clarifies the ontological status of human dignity. By my view, human dignity is not innate in the factual sense of being inborn; rather, it is a rationally constructed moral metaphor for innate properties. I shall draw on the work of Lawrence Kohlberg to defend my view of dignity's universal rational construction. I shall also construct a complex theory of the dual ontological structure of natural rights to accommodate the discrepancy between dignity's factual non-innateness and its universal possession by individuals. Such rights as our right to privacy and our right to autonomy will be seen as indeed "natural" because the duality of the ontology from which they emerge is composed of factually innate properties and their metaphorically innate, rational, moral representation. The distinction between factual and metaphorical "innateness" is a distinction between what is truly inborn and what is constructed to represent inborn properties. Both senses of innateness are used throughout, although I have tried generally to use "innate" to refer to inborn properties and "inherent" to refer both to inborn properties and to metaphorically constructed properties. Where I use the word "innate" to refer to a metaphorically constructed property, I stipulate its "metaphorical" innateness, as opposed to the factual innateness of physical properties.

In the first chapter, I depict what I call the "parent theory" to my theory of privacy, a theory of the development of natural rights within both individuals and cultures. This development takes as its focal point, though not its starting point, a description of how we construct (from innate properties) and then use (to create rights) a moral conception of human beings as dignified. I espouse a view of natural rights as instigated (not determined) by "pre-moral" (innate) human properties. The first such properties that I consider are physical properties, such as the need for food and shelter, which, conceived as rights, can easily be violated. The second are the innate privacy and autonomy of the mind, which are related to psychological well-being but which can virtually never be fully transgressed. Through our innate tendency to construct a metaphor of human dignity from psychological natural properties, we find theoretical protection not only for privacy and autonomy but also for the requirements of subsistence. This we do through a process of being, self-perceiving, and self-conceiving.

In elaborating this process, I examine both the moral as metaphor and the body as symbol. I defend a radical view of natural rights as both originally created and societally bestowed[7] by developing a cross-disciplinary approach to the dual (factual and moral) ontology of entitlement referred to above. I draw an explicit distinction between "rites of dignity," which comprise the metaphor of dignity and the unchanging (static) norms which represent our duty to preserve dignity, and the "dignity trade," which comprises rights established by arguing, as it were, on the basis of those static norms and symbols. Implicit in this distinction is a distinction between "rites of privacy" (or of autonomy) and "the privacy trade." I shall clarify how these metaphors and norms come about in the first chapter.

Such terms as "rites" (of dignity and privacy) and "sacred self" may seem to have religious connotations that are not explored here. While I do recognize the connotations of these terms, I intend them in their non-religious, or at least non-divine, senses. I refer, for instance, to rites that are "the general or usual custom, habit, or practice of a country, people, [or] class of persons,"[8] and to sacredness that is "dedication to some person or … purpose."[9] I refer, in the "sacred self," to the part of the self that is key to personhood and therefore dedicated to the personhood of its possessor. I am not bothered by the religious tone of the terminology because I think that natural rights conceived in isolation from divinity do evoke a kind of religion of the individual. I use these terms metaphorically.

The picture of the ontology of natural rights herein presented constitutes my moral world-view, or meta-ethical picture. Essentially I see morality as a rational, metaphorical reconstruction of factual reality, a reconstruction that occurs within all individuals, to varying degrees, and that assists us as individuals and as communities in determining answers to the universal fundamental human question of the meaning of human existence. I construe the theory as an ontology, rather than an etiology, of natural rights because, although I speak of a reasoned and causal structure of rights, the ontological status of human dignity, conceived both as metaphor and as the reason for our conception of human beings as right bearers, is the central issue here. While it could be argued that a metaphor cannot be seen as "real" in a way that could empower it to ground entitlement, I defend, with such theorists as Philip Wheelwright, "the ontological status of radical metaphor … [as] a medium of fuller, riper knowing."[10] I argue that the moral conceived as metaphor is not the moral conceived as mere metaphor; rather, it is the moral conceived as a necessary, rational reconstruction of innate facts that both states those facts metaphorically and adds the meaning they have for our lives. Hence the etiology of natural rights includes a dual ontology of natural rights, comprised of innate properties and the moral-metaphorical reconstruction of those properties.

Included in my explication of the "parent theory" is some attention, through examples, to the matter of the status of our right to privacy at each stage of its development. A fuller account of just what rights the theory allots us occurs in my discussion, in the last chapter, of the privacy rights of the individual *vis-à-vis* the state.

My conception of natural rights as emerging from a process that ultimately sees rights as both originally created and societally bestowed renders my theory unique. Although I seek, with other natural rights theorists, a way to defend the universality of rights such as subsistence rights, autonomy rights, and privacy rights, I go about this defence by examining our metaphorical construction of entitlement. Other theorists have taken alternative approaches. Early natural rights theorists saw natural law as "a standard fixed by nature to be discovered and gradually applied by men."[11] I reject this, arguing that humans gradually develop rights through rational means. I argue, with Lockean rights theorists, that "natural rights are the foundation for all ... civil rights,"[12] but reject the notion that we contract for the preservation of natural rights. Rather, I view the bestowal of natural rights upon each member of society, by each other member, as part of our rational metaphorical expression of the meaning of specific innate properties for our lives. I reject all notions that we are born with rights, except insofar as we are born with the innate capacity to construct them. Hence I also reject contemporary views, such as A.I. Melden's view, of rights as inborn due to our membership in a moral community.

The theory I propose is clearly individualist and bears glaring elements of universalist essentialism, the view that we are all alike in essential ways, given that I make claims about the necessity of morality's being constructed in the same way by everyone. Hence it requires defence across disciplines such as anthropology and psychology (with a particular indebtedness to the work of Lawrence Kohlberg) as well as philosophy. This cross-disciplinary defence attests, however, not to the philosophical weakness of the theory but rather to the social, political, and psychological relevance of the issues herein addressed. "Privacy" is a hot commodity at every level of individual and community life, including the international community; so are natural rights. Proving privacy, with autonomy and even subsistence, to be a natural right should spark interest. More importantly, I provide a cross-disciplinary defence of my philosophical claims in recognition of the impossibility of isolating moral philosophy from the world it seeks to describe and define, a world that is also described and defined by historians, anthropologists, and psychologists.

Besides its supportability across disciplines, there is a compelling reason to accept my depiction of the moral world. It works. It works not only to explain our basic confusion about whether we have inherent rights but also to explain and resolve confusions over the right to privacy. Is this right innate or bestowed? It is both. It is non-normatively factually innate and universally culturally bestowed as a right. Is it a political necessity or a social luxury? It is a political, social, and individual necessity where it truly reflects the human dignity that grounds it. "Privacy," as a social luxury, occurs only where the "sacred self" is extended beyond its genuine connection to dignity; but in that case, privacy is arguably not the luxury in question.

The answers provided to these fundamental questions may not, at this point, be clear, but my goal is to establish that the answers are present within my theory of natural rights and of the right to privacy. In defending specific aspects of my theory in the second, third, and fourth chapters, I explain and reject the view that privacy is a negative form of freedom and other reductionist views of privacy, natural rights theories that see human dignity as factually innate (and that therefore view rights, such as our right to privacy, as given in individual biological birth), and historical theories that see privacy as a luxury reserved for materially advanced societies. I also demonstrate the inadequacy of earlier attempts to ground privacy in human dignity. These are the theoretical discrepancies herein resolved.

In the second chapter, I provide a deeper analysis of privacy and autonomy as the natural properties that evoke, universally, a metaphor of human dignity and that are reflected again in the manifest rights that emerge from that conception as symbolic protections of it. Before starting, I distinguish the "rights trade" as the fifth level in the ontology of rights, the level that consists of the trade in rights that are said to be grounded in the cultural ideology of dignity. I distinguish the trade at this point because a critical function of my analysis of privacy and autonomy is the exposure of an interdependence between them that is present not only at the factual-innate level (pre-morally) and within dignity (moral-metaphorically) but also at the post-bestowal, or "trade," level at which privacy and autonomy often seem to be opposed to one another; for one person's privacy, at the social level, is always getting in the way of another's autonomy, and vice versa. The existence of this interdependence, hidden in such interactions, in conjunction with their apparent opposition, is what leads to the view of these two entities as inversely identical, i.e., to a view of privacy as negative freedom. I demonstrate, however, not only that privacy and autonomy are distinct at all levels of their development into rights but also that at the trade level, theirs is an interdependence of necessary social ideals born of necessarily innate properties, rather than an interdependence of negative identity.

In the third chapter I defend the theory against anticipated objections. I rebut the charge that I commit the naturalistic fallacy and I defend both my use of an ideal of personhood as the source of moral obligation and the universalist essentialism inherent in my theory. The role I claim for the universal moral conception of human beings as (metaphorically) innately dignified emerges as the pivotal issue in my defence. Lawrence Kohlberg's findings and theory on the matter of human moral development are critical, especially insofar as his work supports my view of human dignity as universal, rationally constructed, metaphorical, and as the origin of the moral.

Because I use Kohlberg's ideas to support mine, and because he seats autonomy alone, rather than autonomy and privacy, with human dignity, it is necessary that I re-defend the role I claim for privacy as both distinct within and integral to our conception of human dignity. Thus, in the fourth chapter I distinguish privacy as an element of the factual (pre-moral) and the post-bestowal (trade) level of the ontological structure of natural rights by rejecting both the reductionist view of privacy and the view of privacy as an interest that emerges within specific cultures only. By rejecting the latter view, I deepen my defence of the individualist bent of my theory and conclude my evaluation of selected but representative elements of the theoretical literature about privacy.

Granted, I do not evaluate all strains of privacy theory, nor do I engage a broad range of literature on natural rights. Rather, I address those theories that I see as most opposed to or supportive of my own, in an attempt to render a clear account of the meta-ethical picture expressed in my theory of the dual ontological structure of natural rights and of our natural right to privacy. Space prevents me from entering fully into the debate between Lawrence Kohlberg and Carol Gilligan on the matter of "justice versus care"; clearly, my use of Kohlberg's work and the limited universalist essentialism that I endorse suggest that, on the whole, I accept Kohlberg's argument that justice and care need not be mutually exclusive in a stage model of the development of moral reasoning.

In the fifth chapter, I turn to the most important ways in which my theory works. It provides a basis upon which to gauge the legitimacy of rights-trade claims to privacy (and autonomy, among other things). After a brief discussion of the nature of transgression, I address two specific current trade issues in privacy. I argue that decisions should be based directly upon the degree to which specific claims are grounded in our ideologically deep (or "untradable") rites of privacy and human dignity. Thus, medical data banks do not, in my view, pose a significant threat to our natural right of privacy, while the submission of personal counselling records at trials does pose such a threat. I demonstrate that something more essential than one's name and health history must be known before one's privacy is truly at stake. This is not, of course, to say that other rights might not be infringed in certain uses of medical information, or even that the information might not be used to transgress privacy by some unethical personnel. I argue simply that medical data banks, if access to them is restricted for specific purposes, do not transgress privacy. Personal counselling records, however, bear the status of "innermost thought" and must never be admitted at trials. The chapter concludes with a discussion of how the theory can guide us in resolving the complex question of the privacy of the citizen *vis-à-vis* the state.

My aim here is to depict a workable ontology of the rational construction of natural rights and of our right to privacy. This ontology provides a multidisciplinary theory of privacy that accommodates the complexity of the notion and explains the limitations of earlier views about our right to privacy while providing a way to decide hard cases of entitlement. Beyond this, the book advances discussion of human morality and entitlement by demonstrating their deep embeddedness in the human capacity to represent ourselves and our experience through the construction of metaphor.

# 1 The Ontological Structure
of Natural Rights

There are several common definitions of the right to privacy. Among the commonest are that it is an aspect of the right "to be let alone,"[1] and that it is the right to control certain kinds of information about oneself. Such definitions, however, do not capture the essence of the right to privacy. For to call it "the right to be let alone" is to use a metaphor to define only one aspect of what truly constitutes this right, while to define it in terms of information control is to define privacy by just one concrete example of its effect. Below I shall clarify just what aspects of the right to privacy are reflected in these examples. For now, it is important to emphasize that such commonplace definitions seek to explain privacy as a right (rather than as a state) by telling us what specific entitlements constitute that right.

What constitutes a right, however, is rarely found either in a general statement of the "essence" of entitlement or on a list of what falls under the right. It is found, rather, in the process that brings us the right. The process that produces a right to privacy will be shown to possess psychological, moral/metaphorical, and philosophical components, the complexity of which must be understood through the structure as a whole. Understanding this process requires that we first distinguish the right to privacy from a fact or state of privacy, given that some conception of what it is to have privacy must precede any conception of ourselves as possessing a right to privacy.

Thus, the question "What is privacy?" applies to the natural fact underlying our right to privacy. The emergent question, to be addressed here, is the question how a right to privacy has come to be; for, as suggested above, to define a right of this sort is to define a structurally complex process that begins with the individual's sense of just what the state is to which he or she shall claim entitlement. Such a process includes, at its different stages, several definitions of terms, including separate definitions of privacy as a state and as a right. I shall here provide a depiction, rather than a definition, of our right to privacy.

### PRIVACY AS A NATURAL RIGHT

The distinction I have drawn between privacy as a state and the right to that state is a good starting-point to explain my assertion that our right to privacy is a naturally existing (or "non-created") right that is nonetheless societally bestowed. Two significant questions emerge from the exercise of distinguishing the right to privacy from the fact or nature of privacy within the context of that assertion. The first question, answered above, asks why privacy itself is prior to the conception of privacy as a right. The second asks what relation obtains between privacy itself, privacy as a describable, naturally existing property, and privacy as a societally bestowed right. While it may seem obvious that we must know what a thing is before we claim a right to it, the notion must be clearly delineated before the second question can be appropriately addressed.

Why must we know just what privacy is before we can conceive of having a right to it? I suggest that we cannot know whether we have a natural right to privacy, or whether our legal privacy rights are legitimate, without first knowing specifically whether or not it is in our natures to be private. I suggest this because I hold a view of legal privacy rights as grounded in a natural right to privacy that, in turn, is grounded in our innately private natures. While it is my purpose to defend this particular view of the structure of rights, I wish to emphasize that clarity regarding what it is to be private is essential to eliminating the confusion about entitlement in which we are unquestionably immersed.

For instance, someone with no conception of what privacy is might claim entitlement to "privacy" simply because he or she is aware that society recognizes a right to privacy for all its members. In such a case, however, the claim is not so much a claim to "privacy" as a claim to be owed equal treatment with other members of society. Almost always, when a right to privacy is defended, it is done with a specific social context in mind, a specific conception of what constitutes privacy in that context, and a keen sense of the individuality of the person or persons for whom the right is claimed. A public figure, romping on the beach, may claim a right to be let alone by reporters, or patients may claim a right to control who receives information regarding their health. In both cases an individual claims a right to specific kinds of information control regarding the self within specific contexts. In both cases a claim is based on a subjective, pre-existing conception of what constitutes being in a state of privacy given certain circumstances. In both cases, the legitimacy of the claim is debatable.

Is there not a deeper, more objective conception of privacy lying at the root of these context-specific cases? Upon what do we base our conception of people as having a right to privacy? The argument made by Warren and Brandeis (1984), among others, that inviolate personality, or human dignity, or the sacred self is somehow at the core of our right to privacy fails to locate these concepts precisely within the structure of rights. Such failure, at the core of human rights theories, leads inevitably to the failure of such theories adequately to demarcate the limits of human dignity's power to produce such rights as individual privacy *vis-à-vis* insurance companies, the law, and, more generally, the "state." Yet these limits must be clear if a theory of our right to privacy is to be complete.

This vague conception of what it is about people (inviolate personality, human dignity) that grounds a right to privacy neglects the details of the process underlying the right; for, in granting factually innate moral status to the privacy of individuals, such a view makes the right to privacy a naturally bestowed right and renders the study of human moral entitlement a fully metaphysical pursuit. Any view that grants innate existence to any specific rights will have difficulty showing how its moral ontology functions or should function across cultures or in spite of religious or other kinds of beliefs. Yet it is part of the function of a theory of human entitlement to bridge the relativity of morality across cultures.

While the conception of inviolate personality, or innate human dignity, attempts to point to the aspect of personhood that stands as the basis for a specific moral obligation to human beings, it grounds conventional morality in an elusive conception of natural morality. I argue that the conception of people as having a right to privacy is grounded in a moral conception of people as dignified, but I cannot see that such a conception stands as the ultimate factual-ontological, or natural, basis of that right. Rather, a moral conception of people (as dignified) must itself be born of some innate, natural, non-moral, and observable human properties. One such property is the individual's innate privacy, which constitutes the pre-moral, natural privacy that stands at the beginning of the process that eventually elicits obligation towards privacy.

What, then, is this innate human privacy that constitutes the factual, non-moral basis for our right to privacy? In order to answer this question, I must clarify the sense in which I see this innate privacy as the origin of rights. I do not hold the common view of natural rights as being given at birth: I see them as grounded in specific sorts of human properties to which some process of human perceiving and conceiving has allotted moral value. This chapter begins to define specifically what it is to have a "right to privacy" by depicting what it is to have natural rights at all. From this discussion will emerge a clear view of the sense in which our right to privacy is a natural right and of where it fits in the scheme of our natural rights. Answers to the questions of boundaries between individuals and authority structures will also begin to take form.

### THE PARENT THEORY:
### AN ONTOLOGY OF NATURAL RIGHTS

Over a quarter-century ago, Joel Feinberg expressed sympathy with "manifesto writers" who treated the demands of poor nations to have unfulfilled needs met "as if already actual rights."[2] Such demands, he said, regrettably could not be considered "valid claims" because they do not stand "as grounds of any other people's duties."[3] In considering such claims valid we would commit the "naturalistic fallacy" of deriving prescriptions about feeding people from the fact of their needing food. My theory works to legitimate some nature-based claims not by rejecting the validity of the fallacy itself but by presenting a view of the "ought" as constructed upon a moral ideal of personhood that holds an intermediary position between facts and the value we place on them. For Feinberg espoused the conviction that though "basic needs" (presumably the requirements of subsistence) cannot be identified directly with "human rights," they are nonetheless "'permanent possibilities of rights,' the natural seed from which rights grow."[4]

Let me now identify the seeds of rights more precisely and then show how innate facts grow into legitimate rights, or "valid claims," that stand as grounds for other people's duties. The first task is to distinguish the factual content of a natural right from its moral content, or the obligation attendant upon it, in order to describe adequately the complex ontology of natural rights. What sort of properties constitute the seeds of rights? First of all, they are human properties that stand at the "factual" basis, as factual instigators, of the process that gives us many of our bestowed rights. They can be roughly divided into two categories of property, the physical and the psychological, and they ground what I call physical and psychological natural rights.[5] Physical natural rights have to do with meeting the requirements of subsistence. The specific physical properties that are the seeds of this broad category of natural rights include the need for food, the need for clothing (in some circumstances), and the need for shelter. In all humans such physical needs motivate not only the desire to have the need met but also the perception of both the need and the desire to meet it. The fact of these needs, then, motivates a perception of the needs and of the desire to have them met, which is a perception of the factual nature of the self and stands as the primary rational motivator for eventual bestowal of a right to have such needs met.

We are still a long way from that eventual legitimate right that requires bases both in natural facts and in human thinking about natural facts. On the basis of a self-perception of the need for food we can arrive, through rational deliberation, at a model of all people as requiring food and even as desiring food. Such a model, however, is not descriptive of human rights but only of human nature. To develop a right, we must turn to the psychological natural human properties.

Psychological natural rights are built upon properties that are unrelated to physical subsistence but are nonetheless connected with minimal emotional or psychological well-being. Our autonomous and our private natures constitute these properties and are distinct from subsistence properties in that they reflect not only need but also innate fulfilment. For while it is certainly in our "natures" to *need* food and to need, for instance, privacy, it is also always the case that we *have* privacy (and autonomy) in some degree, whether or not we have all the privacy we desire. We are innately private, though we are not innately "fed."

This distinction between physical and psychological natural properties is the basis of an important distinction between the physical and psychological natural rights that are constructed upon them: while physical natural rights (properties of physical need with obligations attached to them) can be fully transgressed with extremely detrimental effects, including the loss of life, psychological natural rights, though they can be attacked and even transgressed, can never be fully transgressed. The ironic significance of this difference is that it enables psychological natural rights to be as fully "innate" as physical natural rights, but in a different way. To understand this, we must look at the relationships between needing, desiring, and having as they pertain to physical and psychological natural properties.

We desire food because we need food, though we do not necessarily have it. Some might say that we desire privacy and autonomy because we need them, though we do not necessarily have them. I say that we desire privacy and autonomy because we "have" them, in the sense that it is in our natures to be private and autonomous, and that, indeed, we do not necessarily need them, in the sense of needing more than we innately have. Although we innately have the degree of privacy and autonomy required for personal identity to subsist, we nonetheless both need and desire to maintain these innate properties.

Because there is no doubt that we need food to live, requiring food is clearly an innate property of humans. Because we do not need privacy and autonomy to live, there is some question whether our need for them is innate. Because we innately have privacy and autonomy, however, as ultimately inviolable characteristics, though we may not need any more, we are nonetheless innately private and autonomous. Hence though physical natural properties are innate needs while psychological natural properties are innate possessions, both are nonetheless innate properties that involve us in needing, desiring, and having. They are thus the perfect natural seeds of rights.

### IDENTIFYING PSYCHOLOGICAL NATURAL PROPERTIES

Were we innately "fed," there would be some identifiable bio-logical system that produces the state of being fed. That we are in-nately in a private and autonomous state requires that there be an identifiable privacy and autonomy about us. I suggest, as I earlier implied, that the privacy and autonomy of thought and especially of the production of thought are, in any context or circumstance, privacy and autonomy in their root forms. The privacy and au-tonomy of thought are what we experience as innate privacy and autonomy, and they are necessary components of psychological self-identity. The privacy and autonomy of thought production we do not experience; they simply are, and they are necessary components of philosophical personal identity.

I do not argue that self-identity and personal identity are de-finable as the psychological natural properties of privacy and autonomy. Rather, I argue that those properties are necessary components of self-identity and personal identity respectively, because they are required to preserve both sorts of identity, how-ever we may define them. I distinguish the privacy and auton-omy of self-identity from that of personal identity in order to illuminate an important distinction between our awareness of in-nate privacy and autonomy and the fact of those properties. For while psychological self-identity requires truly psychological pri-vacy and autonomy in order to survive, the privacy and auton-omy that preserve personal identity, or who we are in ourselves, are not truly psychological. They are physical facts about the function of the brain.[6]

If we imagine what is required to preserve personal identity, conceived as the simple fact of who we are, we imagine what it is that would ensure that we produce our own thoughts. That we produce our own thoughts, however, is not sufficient to define personal identity; it simply allows that we have a personal iden-tity, without saying anything about the fact that all personal identities are different. Even if we were to define personal identity loosely as the production of one's own thoughts in accordance with one's own nature, we have no access, on an individual basis, to the unique nature that makes that personal identity what it is. Individual personal identity, then, is indefinable; we are not aware of our personal identity and do not have access to the production of our own thoughts any more than we have to the production of someone else's. Hence personal identity simply is. It is a philosophical concept.

Having a personal identity entails our possessing at least the minimal privacy and autonomy that are present when a brain functions independently (without interference, that is, from thought-controlling devices). The privacy and autonomy that preserve personal identity, and that are not psychological entities because we cannot make ourselves aware of them, are facts about the independent function of a brain. They are simply natural facts. Yet I have called the innate privacy and autonomy that ground rights psychological natural properties. I have done so for two reasons.

First, in spite of their ultimate status as aspects of people that simply are, being of the unconscious thought-producing brain, the seeds of rights are nonetheless linked to the privacy and autonomy of the mind, "mind" referring to the conscious, substantive thoughts that have been produced. Were individuals engaged in the psychological (mind) pursuit of defining their self-identity they might indeed, however futile the effort, seek access to personal identity, at least insofar as that identity is unique to them; why we produce the particular thoughts we produce, however, is an aspect of the brain's privacy that is unavailable to the mind.

Luckily, the close link between mind and brain, as I have defined them, is not the only justification for labelling the seeds of rights "psychological" properties. Since the innate privacy and autonomy that are the ultimate source of rights are not genuinely psychological in the sense of being involved with thoughts themselves (being involved, rather, with thought production, of which we are not aware), they are themselves insufficient to preserve psychological self-identity, though they are necessary to its preservation. The privacy and autonomy that do directly preserve self-identity are critical to our awareness that our minds function privately and autonomously and, therefore, to the possibility of our constructing a morality of entitlement on the basis of that independent function. So, what is the nature of the privacy and autonomy of thoughts, especially as it provides protection for self-identity? Note that I shall refer hereafter to the privacy and autonomy of the "mind," while recognizing that the ultimate seeds are of the brain.

There is a large body of empirical psychological data that supports my conception of the privacy and autonomy of thought as necessary to the preservation of self-identity, as I conceive it. In particular, studies of the effects of sexual abuse on children have demonstrated conclusively that when the privacy and autonomy of the body and even, to a degree, of thought are violated, the mind goes elsewhere. These studies point specifically to the phenomenon of "dissociation," which "may be manifested in disengagement (or 'spacing out') during times of stress, detachment or numbing, out-of-body experiences, repression of painful abuse-related memories, fugue states, and multiple personality disorder."[7] Such long-term effects have been shown to begin as the initial response to the abusive act itself: "During sexual activity, the most common responses were dissociative reactions ... Fifty-one percent (51%) of the respondents reported leaving their bodies, and 40 percent ... reported observing themselves from nearby."[8]

In dissociating from the body that is being violated, victims manage to sustain the privacy and autonomy of thought, or of psychological self-identity. Hence while egregious violation has occurred, it is in the nature of humans that full violation has not occurred. Indeed, these examples demonstrate the function of psychological privacy and autonomy to preserve self-identity, which must itself be fully violated before personal identity can be placed at theoretical risk. The relationship between the privacy and autonomy of thought and the privacy and autonomy of thought production is thus critical to our capacity to construct rights. In the fact that we are able to seek refuge from violation within our thoughts themselves, we can become aware of our natures as innately private and autonomous. I shall later argue that it is on the basis of such awareness that we construct a conception of ourselves as entitled to privacy and autonomy.

In spite of the fact that their association with innermost thought and thought production leaves psychological natural properties ultimately inviolable, were innermost thoughts somehow to be violated, the result would be the erasure of psychological self-identity. By the same token, were the independent production of our thoughts to be transgressed, the erasure of personal identity would result, just as starvation eliminates the body. The importance of morality for the protection of individuals is reflected in the fact that the "self," like the body, can become quite thin and ill without being completely erased. This is evidenced in the possibility of self-identity's being erased, though personal identity remains intact. We can be who we are without knowing that we are ourselves. Before addressing that point in the factual ontology of natural rights at which their moral ontology begins, I must first elaborate the inviolability of psychological natural rights (in their pre-moral phase as properties) through a thought experiment.

## THE INVIOLABILITY OF PSYCHOLOGICAL NATURAL RIGHTS

Is it truly inconceivable that psychological natural rights cannot be fully violated in the way that an established right to eat might? While sources in psychology support this claim,[9] my chief defence is a philosophical argument that begins with the above-noted association of innate privacy and autonomy with one's innermost thoughts. Even if we were to imagine something as extreme as Wasserstrom's "thought-violation machine," which could discern and expose all the contents of a person's mind,[10] the machine would have to work constantly in order to violate fully a person's privacy. Moreover, there is an argument to be made, in this case, for the ultimate inviolability of innate privacy in the fact that the thinking mind will, as still-autonomous producer of the thought, always be a "step ahead" of the violation machine. In this immeasurably small moment of decided autonomy is also situated the inviolable, innate privacy of the individual.

The temporal metaphor is intended to refer not to the nanoseconds of privacy and autonomy that are preserved between the production of thought and thought itself but rather to the distinction explained above, between the preservation of personal identity and the preservation of self-identity. The thought-violation machine can indeed utterly transgress self-identity by usurping any awareness we may have of ourselves as independent beings with private and autonomous thoughts. It cannot, however, eliminate personal identity, or the simple fact that we are who we are. To do this, as suggested above, the machine would have to produce our thoughts for us. The "moment," then, of decided autonomy, in which is also situated our inviolable privacy, is actually a lifetime, as long as our brains function independently to produce our thoughts. Thus, I do not endorse a view of privacy and autonomy as having perpetually to relocate, as it were, nanosecond by nanosecond; they are a moment ahead not of thought violation but of the actual hook-up to the violation machine.

The question arises once again whether I locate innate privacy and autonomy with "innermost thoughts" or with the pre-thinking state of personal identity itself, and personal identity alone. In general, innermost thoughts will suffice, given the conscious element of the rational construction of rights. Theoretical accuracy, however, when faced with the thought-violation machine, requires that I situate them with personal identity. One might object to this through appeal to the intuitively strong claim that the violation machine, in violating all privacy and autonomy except what constitutes the preservation of personal identity, effectively violates all privacy and autonomy. This cannot be the case, however, where personal identity, or who we are as independent producers of thought, remains intact, though self-identity, or our awareness of who we are, is gone. Just as the starved-to-death body no longer needs or has the capacity to use food, so the violated-to-death identity no longer "needs" or has the capacity for privacy and autonomy; a capacity that all who produce their own thoughts certainly have, though they may be unaware of it.[11]

This is all well and good, of course, until we take the step of constructing the thought experiment in which the violator can indeed produce our thoughts for us. I have said above that in doing so the violator erases personal identity, or the theoretical self, just as starvation eliminates the physical self. But surely one cannot elude the concept of one person's being violated by saying that that person has been erased and made into another person (or no person at all) and that therefore his or her rights cannot be said to have been transgressed. No indeed. And so we see that the ultimate "inviolability" of individual privacy and autonomy of which I speak is not an ultimate theoretical inviolability but rather a commonsense empirical inviolability. In fact there are no thought-production machines and the theory assumes that, for all practical purposes (and most theoretical purposes), human thought production is biologically independent and inviolable.

In reality, innate privacy and autonomy are immeasurably less transgressible than even the first violation machine would allow. It is impossible indeed to think of an individual's privacy being completely violated by either a medical data bank or a peeping Tom, or to think of an individual's autonomy being completely violated by a ban on smoking in public enclosures. In fact, to compare the starved-to-death body with the violated-to-death identity is somewhat misleading, given that the full transgression of privacy and autonomy is merely a theoretical possibility, dependent upon person-by-person (or even mass) exposure to a theoretical violation machine, while mass starvation (to death) is already an established fact. Paradoxically, however, when it comes to examining physical and psychological natural rights from a moral standpoint, I will show that while physical natural rights, which are based on our physical needs, are most vulnerable to violation – and thus most dependent upon the language of moral rights – it is nonetheless the case that obligation towards all potentially right-producing human properties develops from our perception of the psychological properties of privacy and autonomy.

The natural, virtually inviolable privacy and autonomy here identified are the privacy and autonomy with which we are little concerned in our pragmatic dealings with rights. Yet they are the properties that I have identified as both the motivational and the ideological core of pragmatic claims, given that they are the non-moral instigators of the process of creating rights. Moreover, once we have established a "right" to any degree of privacy, we include within that right the protection of the mental privacy (and autonomy) that we have by nature. There are none among us (in Western culture, at least) who would not claim a right to the privacy and freedom of our thoughts and their production; no citizen would accept state interference in his thoughts. Such privacy, then, is both the instigator of a right's construction and what is most stringently protected under the right constructed.

THE IDEOLOGICAL CORE:
HUMAN DIGNITY

Earlier, when speaking of physical natural rights, I suggested that rational individuals, generalizing from the fact that they require food to live, conceive of all people as having this requirement. I said at that time that such perceptions (and the ideas to which they lead) were the "primary rational motivator for eventual bestowal of a right" to food. To conceive of all people as requiring food, however, is not in itself sufficient to establish obligation on anyone's part to provide food. For this, we must turn to psychological natural properties, which are psychological natural rights in their pre-normative innate state, and to the conception of people that is constructed upon our perception of them.

The conception of human beings as requiring food to live, which arises from the fact of our needing food, is not a moral conception; it is the result of physical facts. That this conception functions as the ideological "core" of some models of distributive justice is true insofar as it provides the ideological starting point: human thinking about human nature. It is a conception of human nature that is grounded in a perception of that nature. Obligation towards the starving, however, can come only from a moral conception of human nature. Such a moral *con*ception is constructed upon people's *per*ception of their psychological natural properties, such as innate privacy and autonomy and the desire for privacy and autonomy, because of the sense these properties give of the extra-physical nature of human beings. I claim that the moral conception of humankind that arises directly from individuals' thinking about their innate privacy, autonomy, and desires for such is the conception of people as inherently dignified. Moreover, I shall argue that this conception, once it is established in the minds of self-perceivers, functions as a source of obligation towards much more than the specific aspects of personhood that evoke it. First, however, I shall elaborate the connection between innate privacy and autonomy and the moral conception of people as dignified.

The ideal of human dignity and the facts of human privacy and autonomy are all intimately connected with notions of self-control and power over ourselves.[12] By the fact that there is always some part of our thoughts known to ourselves and to no one else, we are self-possessed in the sense of having sole access to certain of our thoughts. Through this, we maintain a degree of power over our own persons in any sense in which exclusive knowledge of one's own thoughts can be seen to provide power or protection. In this lies our innate privacy, a property of all people. One can see how a conception of people as inherently dignified might develop from a perception of this fact of human privacy when one considers that to maintain an appearance of dignity – which, according to the *Oxford English Dictionary*, requires "nobility or befitting elevation of aspect, manner, or style"[13] – we must certainly have the power to conceal any thoughts or aspects of ourselves that might make others see us as undignified.

Of course the moral conception of people as dignified does not arise solely from our innately private natures but also from our innately autonomous natures. Our autonomy also is intimately bound up with our conceptions of self-ownership, self-control, and individual empowerment. While the innate privacy of thought evokes the notion of dignity through the self-control of concealment, its innate autonomy gives us the dignity of agency.[14]

The moral conception of human beings as innately and inherently dignified, then, is what I referred to above when I spoke of the "sense" innate privacy and autonomy give of one's "extraphysical nature." Yet this "sense," or conception, is not exactly of the same kind as the conception of people as requiring food to live that we derive from the apparent need for food. For the conception of people as innately dignified is not based upon a perception of need but rather comes from a perception of something that indeed we have, as a characteristic, and of which we might like more, to nurture that characteristic. It is a moral metaphor for a non-moral fact of non-physical human nature. As such, it has not the initial tangible reality of a conception of people as requiring food to live; indeed, we are not innately dignified. We are innately private and autonomous; when we perceive ourselves as such, we develop a conception of ourselves that metaphorically reflects the nature (as related to self-control) and innateness of those properties.[15]

Once in place, whether in the psyche of the individual or in the morality of a culture, the "innateness," metaphorical or not, of human dignity functions to protect us not only against the indignities of thought violation (or other of life's indignities) but also against the indignity of certain kinds of death, such as death by starvation in a world of plenty. For although dignity is not originally innate, once constructed, it is factually inherent. Obligation, then, with regard to physical natural properties is constructed upon the moral conception of personhood that stems from psychological natural properties. But I have not yet clarified how obligation, which gives the conception of humans as dignified its "protective" powers, arises from such a moral conception of humans. For this we must look at individuals both in themselves and in society.

## DIGNITY AND OBLIGATION: SEEDS OF THE MORAL ONTOLOGY

The point at which obligation with regard to privacy and autonomy enters the process of forming rights is the point at which societal self-conception emerges from individual self-conception. While theorists can be found who view privacy and autonomy rights as both bestowed and created by community, they do not account adequately for the tenacity with which humans stake a claim to these rights.[16] Neither would such claims, were they culturally created, be likely to appear as universally as they do.[17] If indeed the emergence of such rights as our rights to privacy and to autonomy were strictly a function of cultural development, created, that is, through the nature of culture, it would be difficult to explain how it is that these rights exist in different forms, expressed through different norms, in virtually every culture. Something common to all people in all cultures underlies the emergence of rights.[18] My earlier account of psychological natural rights accommodates such tenacity and catholicity by demonstrating a source in innate nature and self-perception for the creation of these rights.

Interestingly, however, were we to view these rights from the standpoint of theories that see fundamental natural rights as originally connected to obligation, we could not adequately explain the deep conflicts within a given community over the issue of societal obligation to protect individual privacy and autonomy. Hence I suggest that in spite of the individual's perception that obligation is inherently due innate, personal properties, it is the case instead that cultures bestow these rights upon their members. This is evidenced in the fact that however predisposed we may be, by nature or by our perception of our innate properties, to conceive of ourselves as innately dignified, we are not. Dignity is not an innate property but is, rather, the property that humans *perceive* as innate by thinking about psychological natural properties and what they signify about human nature. Yet it is the "fact" of dignity that entails obligation. A conception of human beings as dignified bears moral implications that the respective facts of people as private and autonomous do not. The latter are natural facts, while the former is a moral characterization of those facts.

Hence we see that it is not human dignity itself but rather the universal tendency so to conceive of people that is the "fact" upon which whole cultures ultimately base bestowal of "the protection of human dignity" as a right. The conception of humans as dignified functions as an intermediary between how we are, as individuals, and the rights we grant ourselves, both as individuals and as a group. It is not merely original, psychological properties that society protects in bequeathing privacy and autonomy rights upon its members; it protects also this emergent conception of people as dignified. It protects an accepted ideal of moral personhood.

## THE METAPHOR OF DIGNITY DEFENDED

Here I shall digress into a defence of the pivotal, metaphorical role I see for dignity in the construction of human morality and rights. Clearly, problems with grounding natural rights have led me to the conviction that all natural rights are both naturally created and societally bestowed. Having arrived at this conclusion, I must come to grips with how it is so: I must develop a theory of natural rights as both innate and constructed.

In reading the literature on natural rights I have found that many writers defend the innateness of certain rights by appeal to a vague but effective notion of human dignity.[19] I believe that this notion is the key to grounding rights, but I cannot find it anywhere "unpacked," as it were, in a way that I can accept. I cannot, for instance, accept that dignity is present in us by human birth alone.[20] The Latin root of dignity, *dignus*, means worthy and is clearly at the basis of our conceptions of human desert and moral prescriptivity. There are those who consider that we are born "worthy" because we are born into moral community,[21] but I cannot see us as being born moral; we are born babies. And if we are not born moral but are simply born into moral community, then where does the moral community originate? I say that it must be rationally constructed and endorsed by its members. Human dignity, or worthiness, is not at the factual beginning of rights; rather, it is constructed from facts to create the moral origin of rights.

I argue here that the conception of humans as dignified is a metaphorical construction. The question arises what kind of metaphor it is, for there may seem to be some discrepancy on this point. Perhaps it is a "radical" metaphor; according to Max Muller, who coined the term, this implies that the root word *dignus* (meaning worthy) is applied to form the name of something beyond worthiness itself. Here it is applied to form the name of inherent human worthiness. Although the root of the word dignity is not used as broadly as some other root terms to produce metaphorical names,[22] it *is* used to form the compound term, "human dignity." This is the name of our inherent worthiness, and it is metaphorical in yet another way.

Calling the conception of humans as dignified a radical metaphor might seem to conflict with the way I have described this metaphor's construction. For I have described its construction as one would the construction of a poetic metaphor. Muller distinguishes a poetic metaphor as one that is formed "when a noun or verb, ready made and assigned to one definite object or action, is transferred poetically to another object or action."[23] He gives the example of when "the rays of the sun are called the hands or the fingers of the sun" where the noun that means hand or finger exists ready made and "is transferred poetically to the stretched out rays of the sun."[24] In describing the construction of the metaphor of all humans as innately dignified I have described a process whereby a conception of what it is for individual humans (such as kings) to display dignity exists ready made and is transferred poetically to the innate biological and psychological properties of privacy and autonomy. I have not focused on the root meaning of dignity and the radical metaphor of human worthiness itself but rather on the superficial meaning of dignity as nobility, honour, and a certain sort of personal comportment. I have said that we call innate privacy and autonomy our "dignity" because both our innate privacy and autonomy and our conception of what it is to appear to be dignified involve our notions of self-possession and self-control. I have done this for two reasons.

The rational construction of morality and moral entitlement, even within the individual, does not begin with the Latin roots of words. The metaphor of human dignity, though it is a radical metaphor, is not initially constructed on the basis of the root meaning of dignity as worthiness. Rather, it is constructed on the basis of a more superficial understanding of the word dignity: we learn the dignity of concealment partly by learning the indignity of the vain emperor in his new clothes; we learn the dignity of agency partly by learning the indignity of slavery and oppression. While I do not mean to suggest that we first learn what dignity is by learning what indignity is, I do mean to emphasize that we learn dignity and indignity together. We learn them often through their symbolic manifestation in norms surrounding the body and personal comportment. Our initial access to the dignity of persons is thus rather superficial; we first see dignity as a thing of the body, or of the visible person.

Because of the concrete, visible nature of our first access to the conception of human dignity, it is plausible to think that the inherent dignity of all people is constructed rationally in terms of this superficial aspect of the term. The innate privacy and autonomy of thought parallel individual control over the veiled and the revealed self. Hence our perception of these properties of thought plausibly leads to the rational construction of a poetic metaphor of humans as dignified. By representing innate properties, this metaphor adds dignity to the innate properties of humans and innateness to our conception of human dignity.

Through this discussion of radical and poetic metaphor I hope to suggest the plausibility of the role I claim for dignity in human morality and to reveal a parallel between two ways of viewing the metaphor of humans as dignified and two ways of viewing natural rights. For just as we must distinguish how we construct the metaphor of human dignity poetically from the construct of the radical metaphor, so must we distinguish how we construct rights, and rationally bestow them, from the construct of innate natural rights. The radical metaphor, "human dignity," represents the conception of human dignity – as indeed innately human – that we arrive at by constructing the poetic metaphor of innate human dignity. The rights that are constructed upon this conception of human beings are likewise poetically constructed, radically innate rights.

A radical metaphor names some object or act according to something it resembles; in conceiving privacy and autonomy rights as natural rights, we name them ("natural rights") according to the innate privacy and autonomy that they resemble, and on the basis of which we construct them. Hence not only is "human dignity" both a radical and a poetic metaphor, so also is a "natural right." Both metaphors possess a poetic element that adds innateness through the likeness of the metaphorical conception to what is factually innate, and a radical element that adds innateness as a fact, through the original meaning of the words in the metaphor. This said, I must add that though natural rights are rational, metaphorical constructions, they are nonetheless genuine rights.

What I have done here is defend the intermediary and pivotal role of human dignity in the construction of morality first through reference to the concept's proliferation in theories of natural rights, where it is often seen as the (somewhat enigmatic) source of those rights. I have explained the enigma of this conception of human beings as being based in the concept's metaphorical nature and defended its strength to ground rights through reference to a view of humans as entities whose capacity for metaphor is an important part of their perception/construction of moral reality. While my arguments are philosophically unconventional, it can, I think, be said that the role and nature I claim for human dignity work to provide a plausible picture of human rights that accommodates human complexity. I present a moral world-view that is helpful to understanding and accepting such human rights as the right to subsistence.

### RITES OF PRIVACY AND AUTONOMY: ON PROTECTING THE INVIOLABLE

To understand how culture is involved in protecting the innate privacy and autonomy of individuals, we must ask: Why should society take measures to protect inviolable, absolute, natural properties? Surely virtual inviolability is its own protection. Any attempt along these lines to vindicate societal inaction would have to ignore the important distinction noted above between the natural creation of psychological natural rights and their societal bestowal. To view the virtual inviolability of our privacy and autonomy as reason to ignore obligation to them is to confuse the impossibility of full violation with the impossibility of partial violation through symbolic transgression. "Symbolic transgression" refers to any actual violation of dignity norms that also constitutes an attempt to transgress the inviolable. Thus, while steaming open someone's mail and hooking him up to the thought-violation machine constitute true violation of dignity norms, both acts also symbolically transgress those innate, inviolable properties that they cannot actually transgress, and that are the seeds of concrete norms. Symbolic transgressions are symbolic, then, only insofar as they represent attempted transgressions of innate privacy and autonomy. They can nevertheless be quite actual transgressions of the norms we have constructed to represent those properties.

To view the virtual inviolability of our privacy and autonomy as reason to ignore an individual's right to them is to confuse our original properties of privacy and autonomy with our bestowed right that attempts shall not be made to transgress those aspects of personhood. In this distinction lies the distinction between non-normative privacy and autonomy as absolute, natural properties that entail no particular obligation and cannot be violated anyway, and normative rights to privacy and autonomy as bequeathed to the individual by society. This is no simple bequest.

For one might ask why cultures opt to attach moral significance to these innate properties through bestowal of rights.[25] We must remember, however, the intermediary conception of human beings as dignified, which, as the first stage in the moral ontology of natural rights, is constructed from the self-perception of psychological natural properties and precedes the cultural bestowal of privacy and autonomy rights. Before such bestowal can occur, a duty to this emergent conception of people must be constructed (within the individual's psyche) to impose meaning, or value, upon innate psychological properties by imposing value upon the metaphor of dignity used to represent them. Once individuals recognize the duty owed by others to the dignity of their persons, they easily generalize from that duty to include the duties of all people to all others. Hence the moral significance of innate privacy and autonomy is not born with the bestowal of rights; rather, both that moral significance and those bestowed rights are born from the individual and cultural perception that innate privacy and autonomy mean something about people – essentially, that people are dignified. Because the metaphor of dignity is a moral metaphor, it becomes necessary to conceive not only of innate privacy and autonomy but also of this emergent view of people as requiring obligation from each of us towards rights, as yet unspecified, of each other.

In anthropological literature it is widely held that all cultures view some kind and degree of privacy and autonomy as essential to effective social interaction.[26] But, as described above, it is not just at the level of social interaction that cultures determine to afford protection to aspects of moral personhood so elusive that they can never be fully violated and so must be protected, if they are to be protected, symbolically. The function of "symbol" (as opposed to the metaphor of human dignity) in the process that constitutes our natural rights can be understood through examples, such as Western culture's symbolic designation of defecation and sexual intercourse as inherently private areas of life, or of unimpeded movement about one's daily business as an inherently autonomous area of life.[27] That these are symbolic designations is evidenced by the well-known fact that some other cultures apply alternative designations to the privacy and autonomy they value.[28] If one accepts my argument that valuing privacy and autonomy stems, in all humans, from conceiving of innate privacy and autonomy morally, as signifying the dignity of persons, then it becomes plain that the cultural differences in the concrete norms that emerge from this process are a function of their nature as symbolic, rather than innate. They symbolize the same innate human properties and way of conceiving those properties and do so through the installation of symbolic norms that are locally absolute, though culturally relative.

Regardless of what areas of life a given culture deems inherently private or autonomous, such designations initially provide two separate protections: they manifestly protect the designated activity, be it intercourse, eating, or going about one's business, and, through that manifest protection, they symbolically protect the inviolate personality, or inviolable psychological properties, of the individual. Both these protections are viewed as protections to which we have a right. It is important to recognize, however, that each concrete, locally absolute, and quite transgressible manifest right to privacy or autonomy (such as the right to defecate privately or to go unimpeded about one's business) ultimately exists because of the psychologically determined (and culturally sanctioned) necessity of symbolically protecting the elusive, absolute, and inviolable natural property of privacy or of autonomy. As shown earlier, this "necessity" arises not from innate privacy or autonomy themselves but from a third entity protected in each instance of bestowal: the ideal of human dignity, which constitutes a moral metaphor for innate privacy and autonomy, and which sees humans as inherently dignified and worthy of dignity.

Hence we have, at the pre-bestowal (though not pre-moral) ideological level, the functioning of a moral metaphor for innate privacy and autonomy and, at the level of the bestowed rights that are manifestly generated from that ideology, the functioning of concrete symbols for innate privacy and autonomy. We see this process at work across cultures, and it constitutes the most basic explanation of the initial moral ontology of natural rights.

One important point is that, while many defenders of the rights to privacy and autonomy have viewed human dignity as the thing protected by privacy and autonomy norms, such a view takes the structure of these rights only as far back as its origins in moral ideology, without looking at the facts about people that evoke this ideology. I suggest that in fact the conception of human dignity functions not only to protect culturally determined, locally absolute privacy and autonomy norms but also, and initially, to represent metaphorically the private and autonomous self that cannot be manifestly violated. Those manifest norms that emerge to symbolize concretely the requirements of human dignity also manifestly symbolize the possibility of making attempts against innately private and autonomous natures. Hence while such norms appear to be privacy and autonomy norms that emerge from the fact of human dignity, they are in fact dignity norms that emerge from an ideology of dignity, itself constructed from a fact of human privacy and autonomy.

So we see that, because humans are viewed as inherently dignified, locally absolute, manifest-symbolic norms are constructed that represent that dignity in the tangible (beyond ideological) realm. These include our defecation, sexual intercourse, and unimpeded movement norms (as well as other cultures' eating norms, for example), which overtly protect the privacy and autonomy of the body or the concrete self. That they do so, however, is not because a conception of the body as private emerges from a conception of humans as dignified but because the body functions as a concrete symbol to represent tangibly the inherent privacy and autonomy of the mind, just as (and so that) the privacy and autonomy norms surrounding the body function to make manifest the ideology of dignity. I shall return to this.

The kernel of what I am putting forth is a point about the ontological structure of psychological natural rights. For just as obligation with regard to privacy and autonomy is bestowed on the basis of our possessing innate privacy and autonomy, so is the conception of the human right of dignity grounded in a conception of humans as inherently possessing dignity. Evidenced by the distinction between a perception and a conception, however, is the fact that our private and autonomous natures are not seated with our dignity but rather are ontologically prior to the dignity that functions for them as a transgressible moral metaphor. This amounts to the claim (made above) that the conception of people as innately dignified is born of the respective facts of innate human privacy and autonomy and constitutes an ideal that many cultures protect through the bestowal of manifest privacy and autonomy rights. These rights, however, ultimately protect not innate individual privacy and autonomy but their "baby": the moral ideal of individual dignity. Hence when we ask on what basis people might claim a right, for instance, to privacy in a public washroom stall, the answer is that our human dignity is at stake. We do not think of our innate privacy being on the line, although that is the ultimate source of our right. This washroom stall example becomes controversial, for some, when we contemplate the rights of a drug-dealing citizen against the state; I shall return to it in my discussion of citizens' rights in chapter 5.

Besides providing metaphorical moral protection for psychological natural properties, then, the conception of persons as innately dignified also stands as a basis for its own (self-reflexive) protection. Because psychological natural properties lead us to view ourselves as inherently dignified, and because human dignity is a *moral* conception connected to moral obligation, we construct upon this self-conception obligation both towards the properties that cause us so to conceive ourselves *and* towards the conception itself.

Thus, the relation between human privacy and autonomy and human dignity is not one of identity but is, rather, both symbolic and interdependent. The conception of innate human dignity is an ideal of moral personhood that both represents psychological natural properties and evokes obligation towards both those properties and the ideal of dignity. Any attempt to protect human privacy and autonomy, which are innately protected, is actually an attempt to protect our conception of humans as innately dignified, which we are not. Rather, we have an innate tendency to construct such a view of ourselves on the basis of innate psychological properties. The grounding of privacy, autonomy, and dignity in notions of self-control makes the "right to privacy and the right to autonomy" the soundest natural "authorities" for the protection of human dignity; inversely, it also makes the conception of humans as dignified the most accurate symbolic "name" for our natures as bearing psychological natural properties.

### STRUCTURAL SUMMARY: NATURAL RITES

Up to this point, I have outlined the first three of a five-part conception of our right to privacy as it is contained in a theory of the ontological structure of natural rights. Through this theory I shall eventually attempt to explain and resolve some of the conflicting opinions regarding this right. At ground level (the start of the factual ontology of natural rights), I have pointed to two distinct types of natural properties that have no obligations attached to them. These include, on the one hand, properties related to the requirements of subsistence (such as our need for food, shelter, and clothing) and, on the other hand, properties that lead to the attainment of minimal psychological well-being, such as innate autonomy and innate privacy. The former, I have noted, are properties that, conceived as rights, can be fully and detrimentally transgressed, while the latter lead to psychological natural rights that, though they can be attacked, can virtually never be fully transgressed. Both sorts of properties constitute profound and universal human desires the fulfilment of which all people pursue. They reflect universal facts about human nature without, however, reflecting any obligation. They are human properties.

The second and third parts of the ontology of natural rights together constitute the most fundamental protections for natural rights, which are entrenched in metaphor and symbolism. Part Two consists specifically of the moral conception of humans as inherently dignified, a conception that functions as a moral/ideological metaphor for innate private and autonomous nature, and upon which is constructed a theoretical moral obligation to preserve human dignity. From this comes Part Three, which comprises both theoretical obligation to protect innate privacy and autonomy, and concrete moral obligations to respect culturally relative yet locally absolute norms. These norms vary, I have said, according to respective cultural conceptions of how "dignity" is best manifestly symbolized. Such norms as our defecation and unimpeded movement norms function within the current theory at both the symbolic and manifest levels. At the manifest level they are concrete symbols of the obligation to preserve human dignity while also, ironically, providing concrete accessibility to the transgression of that dignity. As pure symbols, they represent the societal decision to revere and symbolically protect the innate privacy and autonomy that are non-transgressible facts of human life.

## A DUALISTIC ACCOUNT?
### THE TWO ONTOLOGIES

As diagram 1.1 shows, the fourth stage in the factual ontological structure of natural rights, and the third stage in their moral ontology, is the stage at which we construct the right that the requirements of subsistence be fulfilled. I shall engage this stage through discussion of the role of the body, as separate from the mind, as it functions in the critical foundational stages of original rights, which include our right to privacy. From this discussion will emerge both an analysis of the two ontologies of natural rights, in particular of the right to privacy, and a theoretical basis for defending international distributive justice, or the protection of physical natural rights. While this latter defence is ancillary to my discussion of privacy as a right, it is important in that it completes the theory of natural rights from which the current theory of privacy can be extracted, and because it does so by laying bare the full implications of the body as "symbol" in this theory.

If we focus, for a moment, on cultural differences in the manifest symbolization of the conception of humans as dignified, we soon recognize that, while the specific acts that are protected vary, manifest-symbolic (dignity) norms protect largely the privacy and autonomy of the body. The difference I have noted between the natural rights of the body (regarding food, clothing, and shelter) and the psychological natural rights of the mind may lead

Diagram 1.1
The Dual Ontological Structure of Natural Rights

**FACTUAL ONTOLOGY**

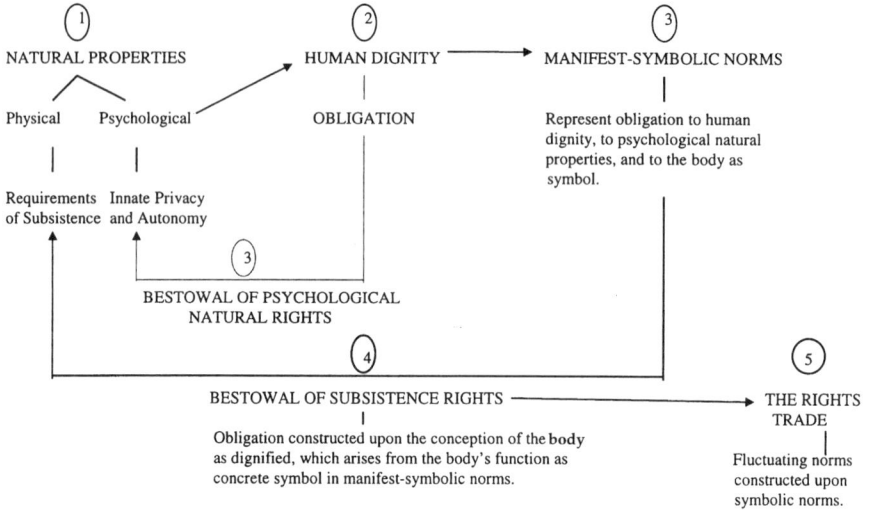

①                           ②                           ③

NATURAL PROPERTIES          HUMAN DIGNITY ———————→ MANIFEST-SYMBOLIC NORMS

Physical    Psychological            OBLIGATION          Represent obligation to human
                                                         dignity, to psychological natural
                                                         properties, and to the body as
                                                         symbol.

Requirements  Innate Privacy
of Subsistence and Autonomy

                          ③

            BESTOWAL OF PSYCHOLOGICAL
                 NATURAL RIGHTS

                          ④                                        ⑤

        BESTOWAL OF SUBSISTENCE RIGHTS ———————————————→ THE RIGHTS
                                                                   TRADE
            Obligation constructed upon the conception of the body
            as dignified, which arises from the body's function as    Fluctuating norms
            concrete symbol in manifest-symbolic norms.               constructed upon
                                                                      symbolic norms.

**MORAL ONTOLOGY**

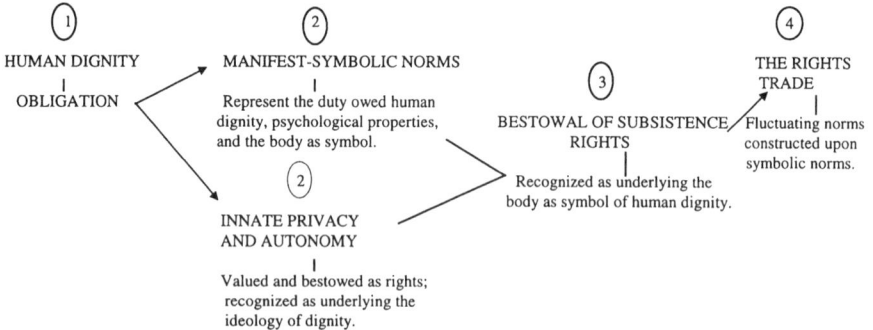

①                           ②                                        ④

HUMAN DIGNITY          MANIFEST-SYMBOLIC NORMS          ③          THE RIGHTS
                                                                    TRADE
OBLIGATION             Represent the duty owed human
                       dignity, psychological properties,   BESTOWAL OF SUBSISTENCE  Fluctuating norms
                       and the body as symbol.                   RIGHTS             constructed upon
                          ②                                                          symbolic norms.
                                                         Recognized as underlying the
                       INNATE PRIVACY                     body as symbol of human dignity.
                       AND AUTONOMY

                       Valued and bestowed as rights;
                       recognized as underlying the
                       ideology of dignity.

the reader to believe that my theory is based in a dualistic account
of human beings. Yet I do not hold the innate privacy and autonomy of thought to be the only "true" privacy and autonomy as
situated in a brain that is somehow the essential seat of personal
identity. I do not hold that the privacy and autonomy of the body
are important only insofar as they both symbolically represent the
psychological properties of the mind and make manifest the possibility of attempting (though not succeeding) to transgress those
properties.

Such egregious adherence to a dualism that views the mind as
essence may seem to obtain because I seem to associate morality
with psychological natural rights exclusively, leaving the nur-

turance of the body entirely to the brutish laws of non-moral nature. I do no such thing, however, for in conceiving of human beings as inherently dignified, we make metaphor (and symbolism) essential to morality. The body as symbol is as integral a part of human morality as is the psychological nature symbolically protected. Moreover, the theory does not preclude a view of the body as being itself both an innate fact – the *sine qua non* of the construction of morality – and the symbol of what we conceive as our worthiness. Within constructed morality the body holds both a pre-moral and a symbolic position. I do not mean, in describing its moral role, to ignore its critical factual role, especially given that the theory builds morality partly upon facts. In conceiving of people as inherently dignified we create a reason to extend moral obligation to all facets, including the physical, of human existence. I shall elaborate the latter point first.

I have claimed that obligation towards physical properties (the right to meet the needs of subsistence) is born of the moral conception of human beings as dignified, a conception we derive from perceiving our innate privacy and autonomy. For this to be the case, we must find in the structure of this right a kind of "working back" of obligation from the symbolic to the innately natural realm. This can be done, in part, from the innateness of our conception of people as dignified, on the understanding that what is both moral and "innate" is strongly situated ontologically to stand as a basis for prescription. Such an approach requires, however, that I address the problem of "innateness," which is evoked by the present theory.

I have distinguished the innateness of the private and autonomous mind from the innateness of human dignity by saying that we are *not* innately dignified but so conceive of ourselves in a way that allows the moral metaphor for innate privacy and autonomy to reflect adequately not just the "control" element of these properties but also their very innateness. This leads, of course, to an ontological paradox in which the moral view of people upon which we base ethical claims (regarding rights in particular) is seen as being both innate and not innate by virtue of being ontologically subsequent to innate properties whose innateness it must metaphorically reflect.

Release from this paradox is found in the epistemological distinctions between being, perceiving, and conceiving, as they relate to the distinctions between nature, the description of nature, and the moral representation of nature. These distinctions are critical to my theory of the two ontologies of natural rights, from which my theory of our right to privacy is derived.

To conceive of ourselves in a certain way, we must first perceive certain inherent facts about ourselves. What we are precedes any perception of what we are, which in turn precedes any conception of ourselves. To conceive of ourselves as inherently private and autonomous beings, we must first perceive our inherent privacy and autonomy. Such a conception describes nature. To conceive of ourselves as inherently dignified, however, is to represent nature morally in a way that places a value upon the thing described and also reflects the desire and the need that such nature should be maintained.

I suggest that indeed all moral representation bears the ontological status of metaphor in that it is always subsequent to what exists in birth while being always originally descriptive of those properties. Metaphors give texture and depth to facts by describing them in new ways. Moral representations give value to facts by describing them in moral ways. So the conception of persons as dignified is, within the metaphysical structure of natural rights, ontologically prior to the *value* of our inherent privacy and autonomy, though it is subsequent to the *fact* of that nature. Moral ontology is the ontology of value in which the viability of placing moral value upon facts about ourselves must precede the specific values of particular facts. Such viability is achieved by conceiving of ourselves in a moral way, as dignified. Arguably, all morality is a metaphorical, perhaps even allegorical, reconstruction of facts we perceive about ourselves. The values we subsequently place on the perceived facts originate in the value-laden metaphors we have used to represent those facts, rather than in the facts themselves. Moral ontology, then, represents a second ontology at work in the philosophical process that brings us natural rights. The "first" ontology is, of course, the factual ontology that includes the introduction of value as its second stage.

Thus, while we are not innately dignified, the metaphorical conception of ourselves as such evokes, through its specific location within the dual structure of natural rights, the moral-ontological priority of self-*value*, arrived at through self-conceiving, over "self" (the facts perceived that lead to self-conceiving). In this way the paradox of innateness is resolved. Moreover, once constructed, dignity *is* inherent (as opposed to innate).

Because the conception of people as dignified is, in a moral sense, ontologically prior to the properties from which it arises, it is morally, though not factually, original. This ontological originality makes it possible to spread value (and therefore duty) back, as it were, from dignity (or forward, on the scale of moral ontology) not only to innate aspects of personhood from which this conception does arise but also to aspects from which it does not directly arise. Such progression is made possible through a combination of two relevant facts. The first is the prescriptive power we allow to any moral aspect of human beings that we view as demonstrably innate. The moral-ontological originality of the conception of people as dignified renders *it* appropriately (though not factually) innate. The second fact is the intimate ontological connection between the innate privacy and autonomy from which our conception of dignity arises and the innate physical properties from which it does not directly arise. Though these properties do not exist in the same way, they do bear the same level of "being," as factually innate properties of people, and are also intimately connected through the body. Hence they are equally viable candidates for the bestowal of dignity-based value, once that value has been established. The allotment of subsistence rights, then, is part of the structural trajectory of the moral ontology at the basis of rights.

In my earlier discussion of human dignity as the ideological core of natural rights, I provided a cursory account of how the metaphorical innateness of this quality, as pertaining to all individuals, functions to invoke obligation to refrain from perpetrating everything from the indignity of thought violation to the indignity of death by starvation. While the above account of moral ontology provides reason to view human dignity as in some sense "original" (being the starting point of value) and therefore as capable of protecting more than the properties from which it is derived, this is nevertheless only one aspect of the duty owed by each of us to the physical natural properties of each other. Indeed, it is the "owing" aspect, and it finds expression in the conception that each human owes a duty to the dignity of each and all others. Why, however, do we owe a duty to the subsistence of the body specifically? Is it not sufficient that we revere the dignity of psychological properties? Given that the body plays two distinct roles in the construction of morality, one pre-moral (factual) and one moral, this question can be answered in two ways. The first, and obvious, answer is that without the body there could be no morality, but this answer does not adequately explain the moral reason for respecting the body. An answer can be found in the significance of the body's symbolic role of concretely representing the innate privacy and autonomy of the mind.

### DUTY TO THE BODY: AS SYMBOL AND OBJECT

The factual ontology involved in the structure of our natural rights (and of our right to privacy as a psychological natural right) moves beyond its second-stage moral determination of value (through the conception of humans as dignified) to the representation of that valuing in concrete (symbolic) rather than metaphorical terms. The valuing represented is, as suggested above, the self-valuing of innate privacy and autonomy, the valuing of these properties in others, and the corollary cultural valuing of innate privacy, autonomy, and emergent dignity of all persons. Concrete representation of such valuing comes in the form of manifest-symbolic dignity norms (called "privacy" or "autonomy" norms) that tend to revolve around the body as intimately connected with and containing the elusive thing that is valued. Also noted above is the fact that the body, as representative of the intangible dignified self, provides the theoretical opportunity for transgression that is required in order to enforce the notion that attempts to transgress are prohibited.

The body (an element of the third in a five-stage factual ontology) is a critical player in the bestowal of dignity rights. That these rights are clothed in the language of privacy or of freedom and in conceptions of the body as private, or as free, is a function of the body's inherent physical connection with what is protected and therefore of its ability to represent those things tangibly. There is also, however, an intimate ideological connection between the conception of dignity (that both grounds and is protected by conceptions of the body as private and free) and the innate privacy and autonomy that constitute what is ultimately protected. The "intimacy" of this ideological connection is the intimacy of cause and effect: innate privacy and autonomy are what *cause* us to conceive of humans as innately dignified. It makes sense, then, that what emerges from that conception might also be clothed in the language of privacy, or of freedom.

It is important to note explicitly that the second stage of the factual ontology of natural rights, in which we both conceive of humans as dignified and construct obligation from that conception, constitutes the first stage in the moral ontology, in which we place moral value on innate privacy and autonomy. While the conception of humans as dignified functions within the factual ontology (as its second stage) to represent innate facts in an ideological, moral metaphor, concrete norms surrounding the body function within that ontology to represent tangibly the valuing of the innate privacy and autonomy of people; in other words, they represent tangibly the ideology of the second stage. Such norms also function, however, within the moral ontology to represent (or symbolize) concretely the "dignified self" that is both created and protected by the conception of humans as dignified with its attendant obligation not to violate dignity. Hence manifest-symbolic norms surrounding the body (such as defecation and clothing norms) stand as the second stage in the moral ontology, though they are the third stage in the factual ontology. Furthermore, although they come second in the moral ontology, these norms nonetheless share this ontological status with the value we place in inherent privacy and autonomy (see diagram 1.1 above).

The value we place in the privacy and autonomy of the body could not possibly precede the value we place in innate privacy and autonomy, because innate privacy and autonomy are the factual origins of our coming to value the body morally. So, when obligation is "distributed" from the conception of humans as dignified, it is spread simultaneously to the origin of the moral conception itself (psychological natural properties) and to the body as representative of those properties. Any sense we may have, psychologically, that the privacy and autonomy of the body ontologically precede conceptions of the mind as private and autonomous could well come from the fact that the body, as concrete, is more easily violated than the mind. This, however, is precisely what renders the body so important as a symbol of what we value in the privacy and autonomy of the mind. Though "second" in the moral ontology of natural rights, the innate properties of the brain and mind may well remain the ultimate seat of identity and are still the factual origins of valid claims; it is the value and nurturance of those properties that are dependent upon an obligation to human dignity that both precedes the value of innate privacy and autonomy and simultaneously extends that value to the body.

To understand that a theoretical universal duty to preserve human dignity includes a duty to respect the body, we must distinguish the specific symbolic functions of the body, within the structure of natural rights, from the functions of the norms that are constructed around it. Indeed the body stands as an "object" within two blended ontologies and functions slightly differently within each. It is an object that a moral ideology of human dignity can use to symbolize visually the seat of personal dignity, and it is a factual object around which symbolic norms can be constructed to symbolize the moral value we place in innate privacy and autonomy. Hence in the moral ontology the body is a visual symbol: a moral, and symbolically sacred, entity; in the factual ontology it is an object to use for the expression of ideology and the bestowal of rights. It is also, of course, that without which there could be no life and, therefore, no morality.

Clearly, then, the body is integral to the development of privacy and autonomy rights (among other natural rights), not only as a concrete extension of the mind but as a focal point for the implementation of ideology that is based in elusive psychological natural properties. The norms constructed around the body to express our ideology of personal dignity also have the effect of applying that ideology to the body, which is the only object around which our ideology of personal dignity can be built. That the body is inseparable from the expression of the right to dignity through the construction of manifest-symbolic norms causes the right to dignity to apply not only to the innate psychological properties that instigate it but also to the body in its initial state. It is thus defensible to suppose that the obligation that attends our conception of humans as dignified bestows rights not only with regard to the psychological properties from which that conception arises but also with regard to the physical requirements of subsistence. The "establishment" of such a natural right bears implications both for international justice – the right of the starving people of other nations to be fed – and, somewhat less controversially, for the right of citizens against the state to be granted the requirements of subsistence where they cannot attain them for themselves. This is not, of course, a privacy right; in chapter 5 I will touch on the implications of the "body-as-symbol" for our privacy rights against the state.

This completes Part Four of my theory of the ontological structure of natural rights, in which the duty owed by each of us to the dignity of each other is a duty owed not only to a general conception of humans as dignified but also to the specific dignity of the individual, the dignity of an innately private and autonomous self, the dignity of the body that both contains and represents that self. I have thus also arrived at answers to the initial queries of this section: whether the innate privacy and autonomy of thought are the only "true" privacy and autonomy, given a theory that seems to see the mind as the essential seat of personal identity, and whether the privacy and autonomy of the body are valuable, on this theory, only insofar as they both symbolically represent the properties of the mind and make manifest the possibility of attempting (though not succeeding) to transgress those properties.

On the basis of these arguments, I conclude that while innate privacy and autonomy are indeed situated in the brain and mind, the body is equally important both in establishing the legitimacy of natural rights and as a specific entity protected by such rights; for while the factual ontology of natural rights finds the innate privacy and autonomy of the mind to be prior to any conception of the dignity of the body, their metaphorical moral ontology extends the duty owed both the ideology of dignity and psychological natural properties (privacy and autonomy) to the dignity of the body, which is inseparable from what is initially protected and functions as a concrete symbol of it. In the second chapter I shall distinguish more fully the psychological properties of privacy and autonomy, and the specific rights that emerge from them.

### SUMMING UP

At the outset I listed two questions that arise from the distinction I make between the right to privacy and the fact of privacy and the bearing this distinction has on my conception of the structure of this right as non-created but societally bestowed. The first question – Why is privacy prior to our conception of privacy as a right? – had to be answered before I could adequately address the second: What relation obtains between privacy itself, privacy as a describable, naturally existing property, and privacy as a societally bestowed right. In this chapter the "priority" of "privacy itself" over privacy as a right has come to be understood as an *ontological* priority in nature. We possess innate privacy and autonomy as natural properties the perception of which leads us, universally, to conceive of ourselves as inherently dignified. Within this factual ontology is a separate, though integrated, moral ontology in which the sorts of values from which we derive rights are shown to be ontologically prior to any value we place on innate properties.

It is through my conception of natural rights as constituted by a complex process that requires the interdependency of two ontologies – the factual and the moral – that I have begun to explain the relational structure of our right to privacy. The distinction between "privacy itself" and privacy as a "describable, naturally existing property" might seem to be a non-distinction on the model provided since surely both terms apply to the innate privacy at the basis of the factual ontology. These terms can, however, with "privacy as a right," be distinguished through the distinction between being, perceiving, and conceiving. Just as what we are precedes any perception of what we are, which in turn precedes any conception of ourselves, so privacy itself, or the natural state of being private, precedes the perception of that private nature and of its requirement of nurturance. So "privacy itself" is privacy that simply is, while "privacy as a describable, naturally existing property" is innate privacy perceived. This, then, is how an innate property comes to be the legitimate original "seed" of a valid claim: it does so through human thinking about human nature and through the universality of the human tendency to construct meaning upon perceptions. Such perception is non-moral (or, at least, pre-moral) because it does not in itself necessitate anyone's obligation to protect the property perceived.

It does provide, however, the cognitive move to a moral conception of the self so perceived. Privacy "as a right" is constructed upon the moral conception of humans as dignified; but it is constructed this way indirectly, because it is constructed from the obligation that, in its turn, we have constructed upon that moral conception. Hence the legitimacy of the right to privacy does not correspond exactly to "privacy conceived of" (as opposed to "privacy perceived," or "privacy itself") but is, rather, constructed upon a conception and therefore bears the status of something "bestowed." While the initial bestowal of this right still belongs within "rites of privacy" (and autonomy), as something under-taken by all cultures, it does not belong to the realm of what is "innate." One might argue that on the present theory all individu-als and cultures come to conceive of human beings as innately dignified, and therefore that to conceive of people in this way is an innate property of individuals. Nevertheless, the symbolic norms that manifestly state the existence of a right vary from culture to culture. Hence these norms and the legitimacy of the claims they stake are bestowed. No innate thought process tells us that certain body parts and activities are inherently private. Moral "conceiving," then, is transitional between what is natural and what is bestowed, providing a conception to which we are des-tined to come, and from which we derive value and the bestowal of natural rights.

Also promised at the outset was a clarification of just what aspects of the right to privacy are reflected in two overly limited definitions of this right: the claim that it is the "right to be let alone" and the claim that it is the right to "control information" about oneself. Of the former definition I said that it constituted a metaphor for only one aspect of what truly constitutes this right. I have not yet arrived at the point in the structure of the right that is reflected in this metaphor, for the "right to be let alone" refers to the right to live a private life and is an element of the post-ritual privacy trade (or the broader "rights trade," which encompasses the right to live a free life). This I shall discuss briefly in chapter 2 and more extensively in chapter 5.

To define the right to privacy in terms of information control is, I have said, to define it in terms of a concrete example of the be-stowal of this right. Some instances of the bestowal of information-control rights may be readily traceable to the ritual bestowal of privacy as a right and may thereby be legitimated through connec-tion to what is absolute about the right to privacy. Other instances of information control, however, will be found to result from the bestowed rights of the privacy trade and may or may not be link-able to the initial structure of natural rights; hence they may or may not be legitimated. Resolution of concrete issues in privacy bestowal will also be addressed later, with reference to specific types of information within specific contexts. I turn now to the matter of distinguishing privacy and autonomy as psychological natural rights.

# 2 Distinguishing between Privacy and Autonomy

In order to depict our right to privacy, the distinction between the two psychological natural rights of privacy and autonomy must be clarified. I must delineate more comprehensively the last stage in my ontology of natural rights, namely, the "rights trade" of post-bestowal society. This is the stage at which we fight for specific, concrete rights and the context in which we formulate our first questions about the nature of rights. It will also be necessary to unravel some of the theoretical controversy surrounding privacy as a right, commencing with the theory, popular in some circles, that privacy is really just a form of freedom. This is a version of philosophical reductionism, rather than legalistic reductionism of privacy to other legal rights – an issue I address in chapter 4.

## THE RIGHTS TRADE

We first understand our rights to privacy and autonomy as they function in the daily workings of society, in the law, in politics, and in our relationships. Viewed from this perspective, psychological natural rights are viewed as they exist in the post-bestowal "rights trade" of Western culture. In order to understand the forthcoming discussion of both the distinction between and the interdependence of privacy and autonomy, we must first understand each of the levels at which privacy and autonomy operate. Thus far I have identified three of four such levels: the "innate" level at which privacy and autonomy are facts, the moral-metaphorical level, in which those facts cause us to formulate a conception of humans as dignified, and the manifest-symbolic level, in which they, with the conception of human dignity, provide culturally relative (culture-specific) yet locally absolute norms that both symbolize and make manifest the ideology of dignity. That these norms are locally absolute renders them "static," unchanging norms within the culture that has established them. At this manifest-symbolic level of privacy and autonomy rights the body is a symbolic object around which dignity norms are constructed. The body's symbolic role, at this level, leads to the prescription of concrete dignity norms that protect the body as well as human dignity. The bestowal of physical natural rights, then, is directly related to the construction of manifest-symbolic norms that preserve human dignity. These three levels of the structure of rights – the innate, the moral-metaphorical, and the manifest-symbolic (with its emergent static norms) – constitute the universal development of natural rights and so can be characterized as the "rites" of human dignity. This process of the construction of rights occurs universally (a point I shall further defend in the third chapter) and stands at the basis of the fourth level at which privacy and autonomy function within the development of rights: the level of the "rights trade."

This trade, to which I have previously alluded, is different in kind from the other three levels where we find privacy and autonomy connected. It comprises norms that are both culturally and locally relative. By this I mean that they are not like our defecation and unimpeded-movement norms because they are not absolute. They can be waived and even taken away.[1] Hence they are societally non-static, or "fluctuating," norms that, although they grow out of and depend on symbolic norms and ideals, are nonetheless established through legal, political, or otherwise social means of making and defending claims. As noted, such claims are often staked on the same ideal of dignity that grounds static norms but are not as evidently connected to it as symbols. One example of such a fluctuating norm is the right to absolute confidentiality in a patient/counsellor relationship. Once someone can show that such a right can be overridden by some other right, the right disappears for a given set of circumstances. Anyone who wants the right re-established for that set of circumstances must either go to court to prove the legitimacy of the right in law, or lobby the government to reform legislation. In this sense, a fluctuating right is both a right for which we fight and one that may be "traded" for some other common good.

Many fluctuating norms are expressive of the privacy and autonomy of individuals as such properties are valued through the moral conception of human beings as dignified. The freedom to report matters of public interest and the right to privacy in childbirth are examples of fluctuating norms that bear very different degrees of connectedness to our universal expression of dignity. Childbirth is so closely linked to symbolic norms surrounding the body that it would be almost universally accepted as something for which one *can* demand privacy, though few do. Privacy in childbirth, as a norm or a right, is distinguished from symbolic norms by being waivable. Indeed, it generally *is* waived to allow the presence of partners, midwives, doctors, or nurses. It is generally *not* waived, or "traded," to allow the presence of curious onlookers from the street.[2] The freedom to report matters of public interest is a still more fluctuating norm, not so much because anyone denies such freedom as because we disagree on what qualifies as a matter of public interest. Note that fluctuating rights can be "traded" either in the sense of being waived, by individuals, to attain other goods, or in the sense of being overridden, by the state, to attain some social good.

SCHOEMAN'S TWO TYPES OF NORMS

I am not the first to distinguish static norms from fluctuating norms, though I may be the first to use these terms. Ferdinand Schoeman, speaking of privacy norms only, distinguishes "two discrete usages or roles of our notion of privacy that are not differentiated in the burgeoning literature."[3] I shall explain these two usages presently. First I must describe part of Schoeman's goal, which is to employ a historical perspective towards the development of a social theory that explains why "the identification of the right to privacy with the right to be left alone is ... incomplete and misleading [in that privacy] functions to protect people in ordinary social contexts, while leaving them open to appropriate levels of social ... pressure ..."[4] While I shall later criticize Schoeman's view that the desire for privacy is strictly a social construction, I nonetheless agree with the general distinction he makes between types of privacy norms.

Schoeman points to two overlapping sorts of norm, both of which relate to our conception of people as dignified, or sacred, and both of which "are reflections of social structure and symbolism."[5] Those that correspond to my manifest-symbolic norms, such as our static defecation norms, Schoeman describes as being "norms that control."[6] He distinguishes these from privacy norms that promote a "private life and freedom from social control"[7] by "facilitat[ing] intimate or personal opportunities otherwise not available."[8] Norms that control "express respect for human dignity by protecting us from public association with the beastly, the unclean."[9] Thus, norms that I view as manifestations of obligation to preserve a conception of people as inherently dignified, Schoeman views as manifestations of "a rigid and internalized form of social control."[10] So what's the difference?

Well, in defence of the notion that what I call static norms are intended as social control mechanisms, Schoeman refers to Stanley Benn's claim[11] that norms surrounding bodily functions (my static norms) "often involve notions of shame and impose duties on us not to present certain facets of ourselves in public."[12] Through reference to Benn, Schoeman hopes to show a connection between the bodily nature of what must be concealed, the shame around instances of exposure, and his conception of those norms as social control mechanisms. While his explicit goal is to illuminate the usefulness of social pressure to our functioning as competent human beings, there is something disturbing about this conjunction of the body, shame, and social control. For whatever his intention might be, what he says here evokes what has become a fairly commonplace explanation of the historical tendency of Western culture (at least) to view the body as shameful: the "social control" explanation.

While the embarrassment currently attendant upon being caught defecating could indeed evoke our sense of shame and force compliance, I nonetheless hold that the social control explanation wrongly tends to leave us thinking that the body is simply put forward as shameful (presumably by people in power) in order that some overarching and multipurpose social control mechanism will be firmly in place when needed, as though the shame attendant upon the body were itself a kind of leash that both symbolizes and manifests the authority of the master, society. I do not suggest that this is Schoeman's view – the shame attendant upon the body in Western culture is not at all the subject of his work – but it is a common view and it is wrong because it presupposes that shame, as a means of control, precedes a sense of obligation in the process that brings us these norms. I suggest, rather, that control (or obligation) is theoretically prior to shame in this process; in order to feel ashamed of our bodies we must first have a conception that human dignity must be maintained. There is therefore a more fundamental "shame" underlying internalized shame about the body. This more basic shame is the shame of "not doing one's duty" with regard to a universally accepted view of human beings. I shall elaborate.

The confusion inherent in the social control view of static norms can be clarified by asking the question "Social control over what?" Schoeman is right to suggest that all privacy norms function to protect human dignity, but he wrongly suggests that the thing specifically controlled by norms is "norm violation"[13] itself. He fails to acknowledge that there must be a reason why norm violation is to be avoided. Of course, proponents of the social control view might misuse Schoeman's claim, arguing that there *is* a reason to control norm violation: to maintain social or political power. This reason, however, steps outside morality into politics and does not account for the moral reasons of those who (in our culture quite fearlessly) obey the norms.

I prefer a less cynical view of human morality (as does Schoeman, ultimately) that recognizes the potential to abuse static norms in the service of politics but sees also both their value in the service of human self-definition and the fact that such norms precede political expediency in the construction of rights and obligations. On my view, however they may be used, static norms are constructed upon a moral rather than a political conception of human beings. The absolute nature of static norms is not lost on this view; any obligation emerging from a conception of people as inherently dignified must be manifestly absolute if it is to reflect symbolically the conceived innateness of that dignity. Innate characteristics, such as our private and autonomous natures (reflected in the conception of human dignity), are absolute. If they are to be protected at all, they must be protected in absolute terms, at some level.

Inherent dignity requires absolute obligation; transgression of absolute duties, then, entails shame in the sense of dishonour rather than in the sense of uncleanliness. The shame attendant upon transgressions of rites of privacy is therefore initially removed from the body, reflecting an established regard for the dignity of the body and of the person rather than Western confusion about cleanliness. It is the shame of manifestly treating people as undignified, not private in nature; it is the shame, once again, of not doing one's duty to a universally accepted view of human beings. So our embarrassment when culturally determined absolute privacy norms are transgressed may well reflect our internalization of conceptions of the body as shameful, but that internalization is a by-product of the specific norms constructed to represent the conception that transgression of dignity (rather than of norms themselves) is shameful.[14]

Hence I agree with Schoeman that manifest-symbolic privacy norms, like other static norms, function as social control mechanisms, but I do not agree that the control entailed by these norms is of a generic and overarching nature: specifically, what is controlled is both the universality of the conception of innate human dignity that arises from our inherently private and autonomous natures and the conception of absolute obligation that such a conception of dignity requires. Unquestionably, the kinds of norm that Western culture has in place to protect its view of dignity can lead to a perception of the body as a source of shame, but such a conception of the body could not possibly be prior to a conception that bodies or people are somehow "above" their functions.

Having distinguished my static norms from Schoeman's social control norms, which are the same norms viewed in a different way, I shall consider Schoeman's "private life" norms. First it is necessary to clarify the distinction Schoeman makes between control norms, which restrict "others' access to areas that are nevertheless highly regulated,"[15] and private life norms, which restrict others' access "with the point of allowing for individual expression."[16] While Schoeman views the former as functioning to bring about the internalization of social norms and taboos, the latter he views as having emancipatory implications with regard to social forces. I have argued that, while there is a control mechanism at work in manifest-symbolic norms, and although they are culturally relative, the static nature of these rigid rules about rigidly defined activities is not so much a function of the need for social pressure as of their primarily symbolic purpose manifestly to represent and uphold a specific conception of personhood. Thus are they static norms. By contrast, Schoeman's emancipatory private-life norms, which are among what I have called fluctuating norms, are primarily pragmatic in function.

For though they are tangible norms bearing practical implications for our daily lives, static norms, as Schoeman points out, have little to do with self-expression or the pursuit of personal flourishing. Fluctuating norms, however, take us a step away from the need to entrench our ideology in our daily living to the pragmatic need to enjoy the rights that that ideology affords us. If we all have an innately private and autonomous inner self that causes us to view ourselves as innately dignified, and if such a view of ourselves causes us to perceive obligations and rights with regard to privacy and autonomy, then it is quite understandable that we should come to view ourselves as entitled, within our social context, to express our private natures (for instance) and dignity through claiming a right to carry on certain aspects of our lives without scrutiny by others. At this point, of course, we have individuals making claims based on their respective perceptions of how social ideology is most accurately manifested, rather than social consensus laying down rules that express that ideology. In the latter case, through static norms, the group speaks to the individual, while in the former case the individual speaks to the group or to other individuals.

To appreciate fully the fluctuating nature of private life norms, we must recognize that "privacy," in this sphere, takes on a slightly broader meaning. It becomes a matter of the whole person's being "let alone," rather than just the inner self that scarcely can be touched anyway. For when we seek a private life in a social context we seek, in a sense, to extend the dignified self to include all that is both visible and concealable about ourselves and our lives. To elucidate the macrocosmic nature of private life claims, one might imagine an entire culture as one person and each individual as a candidate to become that person's innermost self. I think that part of the reason for the extended conception of our private natures may be the fact that across cultures static norms have been related to the body and to bodily functions. The body is, after all, the most immediately tangible representative of our innermost selves, a thing of honour rather than of filth.

So the "big picture" gives us a view of individuals, in varying degrees, as each seeking to be the sacred, inner self of the social structure, each the thing protected by privacy, autonomy, and dignity norms. If Schoeman is right, as I think he is, that culture's absolute privacy norms, like other static norms, function to control individuals (though I do not agree that that is their purpose, given that they come about through a process based in constructed dignity), then he is surely right that non-absolute private life norms, like other fluctuating norms, function to empower individuals, giving them control over both themselves and others. It must be remembered, however, that macrocosmic norms are not absolute, and that even those that become legally entrenched are subject to legal or constitutional rebuttal in the face of privacy, autonomy, or other dignity claims by other individuals or groups. Hence the "societal sacred-self" status of any individual is always on much shakier ground than the innate fact of that person's private and autonomous nature or moral conception of human dignity. While each seeks for his own private or free life the status of an inherently private or free aspect of society, this can never be fully achieved because private or free lives, unlike innermost selves, constantly cross the boundaries of what is inherently public. So in seeking for ourselves a private or free life, we engage in what I call the "dignity trade," or the "rights trade," wherein we stake claims, waive claims in exchange for other goods, and sometimes see claims overridden for the public good. Specific parts of this trade include the privacy trade, the autonomy trade, and the trade in subsistence rights. The level and degree of such trade varies from culture to culture.

## DEBATING THE RELATIONSHIP
## BETWEEN PRIVACY AND AUTONOMY

Having introduced the trade stage, the last in the five-part ontology of natural rights, I can return to my initial observation that this is the stage at which we first encounter privacy and autonomy as rights and the stage at which we begin our attempt to comprehend them. In one way it is unfortunate that what we first see of these rights is the product of the moral-metaphysical development of natural rights because starting here leads many theorists into paradox. The confusion is understandable, though, for the way privacy and autonomy stand in relation to one another within the trade seems beguilingly oppositional. "Beguilingly," I say, because there are, within the ontological structure of these rights, three distinct ways to conceive of this relationship: the initial view of them as opposed; the emergent view of them as inversely identical; and the hidden, though ultimately more accurate, view of them as interdependent, though distinct. The first two views develop as follows.

When we, as theorists, first come to the question just what it is to have a right to privacy or to autonomy, we look for examples and see, in law as well as in the family, that often less of one of these for one person means more of the other for another. We see the privacy of politicians in conflict with the freedom of reporters; we see children's privacy in conflict with parents' freedom (and vice versa). Yet one theorist, Lorenne M.G. Clark, tells us in a very interesting article that "one must be private to be free and be free to be private"[17] and argues that this proves privacy and freedom to be identical to one another; at the very least, if they are not identical, "the one certainly entails the other."[18]

On this view, the trade conflicts between freedom and privacy are seen to be really conflicts between the freedom to act and the negative freedom *from* being acted upon. So while the observable conflicts within the rights trade lead to a view of privacy and autonomy as related through opposition, one of the readiest theoretical explanations of the conflict sees that relation as one of inverse identity. Hence the first two characterizations of the relationship of privacy to autonomy emerge from the tip of the theoretical iceberg that is the structure of these rights. While it is tempting to attribute the paradoxical "opposite sameness" view, which emerges from what we see day to day, to philosophical laziness, it is not hard to see why the "negative freedom" supporters feel their view to be more deeply grounded.

For once we turn from privacy and autonomy as they appear in law, politics, and the trade in general and move deeper into the theoretical underpinnings of these rights, we come to theorists such as Richard A. Wasserstrom who see both privacy and freedom as grounded in human dignity.[19] My own theory (though not really a descending one) might be seen in this way. It is, however, unique in that even when the "dignity theorists" speak of these rights as grounded in "conceptions" of personhood, they nonetheless tend to view the conceptions not as metaphors but rather as acknowledging a dignity that is *factually* innate in humans. While Clark and other proponents of the negative freedom view of privacy reject the notion that our right to privacy is innate because it is grounded in human dignity, they can nonetheless borrow from dignity theorists a conception of privacy and autonomy as unified within one concept or word ("dignity"). I shall return to this unification presently.

The disagreement between Wasserstrom and Clark highlights the potential conflict between the view that privacy is just a negative freedom and the view that privacy is grounded in innate human dignity. Clark argues against Wasserstrom's suggestion that the intrinsic privacy of our thoughts is inextricably bound up with our concept of personhood,[20] and that this is why it is wrong to coerce the disclosure of someone's thoughts. Clark argues that our assumptions about the metaphysical status of human beings are not what lead us to see people as worthy of respect. Rather, it is our "moral judgment to treat people as deserving of respect that leads to our attributing to them areas in which they will be left to their own discretion."[21] Clark would surely hold this objection out to me, as well, arguing the irrelevance of metaphysics to moral custom. Indeed, she tells us that "we could have a concept of personhood such that nothing was held to be private in principle and still treat persons as worthy of respect and as deserving of discretion with respect to some areas of their lives."[22]

Clark fails, however, to describe such a concept of personhood – would it be grounded in dignity, or perhaps utility? – and fails also to see that moral judgments must be made on the basis of moral facts. By "moral facts" I do not, of course, mean original, inborn facts about people, since those are non-moral; I refer rather to socially accepted moral ideals, such as our ideal of human dignity. Clark provides no such "facts," preferring to tell us that rights must be based in "the moral reasons we advance and not on the kinds of things being interfered with."[23] The distinction between my "moral facts" and Clark's "moral reasons," of course, is the distinction between metaphorical facts that are clearly grounded in innate facts and moral "reasons" that are not clearly grounded in anything. So while she is adamant about keeping the metaphysical nature of things out of moral prescription, Clark is nonetheless reticent about providing either the suggested conception of human beings or some other "moral reason" why we might see individuals as worthy both of respect and of a degree of privacy. She is reticent, perhaps, because she does not wish to commit the naturalistic fallacy of deriving "ought" from "is" and thus fails to see that moral facts, the "fact" of human dignity, for example, though born of metaphysical facts, are nonetheless not innate themselves, other than metaphorically. All moral judgments are based on such factually grounded ideals, or principles, and Clark provides no proof either that they are not so based or, the weaker claim, that they need not be so based. I shall return to the naturalistic fallacy in chapter 3.

Having defended Wasserstrom, then, on the matter of linking our concept of personhood with the innate privacy of thought, I must nevertheless lament his failure to see the nature of that link: innate privacy is indeed part of the inviolable source of our concept of personhood. He prefers to see the innate privacy of thought as a part of a plausible concept of personhood rather than as a fact upon which such a concept might be based. While undoubtedly Wasserstrom would see "a core of thoughts and feelings that are the person's alone"[24] as the obvious source of a conception of persons as having such a core, he nonetheless does not make the essential theoretical distinction between what we perceive about ourselves and what we therefore conceive ourselves to be. Without this distinction his argument fails to make explicit the rationale behind his moral claims. Wasserstrom, then, counts among those who provide too vague a conception of human dignity for it to stand as an adequate reason for a right to privacy.[25]

So what I call the "dignity theorists" are those who see human dignity as the ultimate moral and factual core of our rights to privacy and freedom and who neglect, therefore, to explore the factual-ontological foundations of both those rights and that dignity. Often they do not realize that they assume an ontological status for inherent dignity, or that ontology is in any way involved. Thus they see neither the facts of innate privacy and autonomy at the basis of their conception of personhood nor the interdependence of these aspects of personhood at the pre-moral level.

An ascending model of psychological natural rights that begins with the ontology of innate facts and builds to the ontology of value is much better situated to comprehend both the diversity in unity of privacy and autonomy, as definitionally distinct at the metaphorical stage, and their unity in diversity, as interdependent within the macrocosm of the trade, at the stage of fluctuating trade norms. For indeed once we recognize the interdependence of privacy and autonomy at the innate level and understand how that interdependence becomes synthesis at the metaphorical level, we are well situated to recognize the initially hidden macrocosmic interdependence of these properties on the scale of ideals that society upholds and to which society appeals in deciding hard cases. The macrocosmic (trade) interdependence of privacy and autonomy, which I shall defend in this chapter, is hidden from view in the sense that the properties of privacy and autonomy at the trade level seem, initially, to be opposed.

## REJECTING THE "NEGATIVE FREEDOM" VIEW OF PRIVACY

Proponents of the "negative freedom" view of privacy mistakenly equate privacy and negative freedom. They are mistaken in thinking that there is nothing "intrinsically" private, no privacy "by nature." I propose that this mistake is brought about by their confusing the identical *ontological* status of privacy and autonomy – the fact that they exist at the same factual-ontological level – with a kind of identical *definitional* status whereby they are taken to be the same thing. I hold also, however, that this mistake is pardonable given that until now no one has distinguished factual ontology from metaphorical, moral ontology.

At first glance, my theory may appear to support the negative freedom view of privacy at least insofar as it seems, at some level, to see privacy and autonomy as unified. I have, after all, argued that while inherent privacy leads to the notion of dignity through the self-control of concealment, inherent autonomy gives us the dignity of agency, which argument makes it clear that both are forms of dignity (though not of freedom), one being an active and the other a passive dignity. While this may seem to parallel the notion of positive ("active") and negative ("passive") freedom,

freedom is nevertheless not that of which I speak in comparing privacy and autonomy as sources for and forms of dignity. Indeed, I speak of dignity, in particular of the metaphorical, moral conception of persons as dignified. That privacy and autonomy together form the two major aspects of that conception does not require that they be identical, much less that they both be forms of freedom.

The error of the negative freedom theorists, then, is potentially twofold. For those who look only to the empirical evidence of the rights trade, rejecting appeals to innate privacy or dignity as sources for understanding these rights, error results from being overly practical through refusing to explore theories about the underlying moral and natural structure of rights. For those who are willing to accept, in addition to their view of privacy as negative freedom, that our right to privacy is grounded in a theoretical conception of human beings as dignified, error comes from seeing the unification of privacy and autonomy within such conceptions as proof that privacy and autonomy are the same thing. This error results from the failure of theorists thus far to recognize that the moral conception of humans as dignified does not stand as a fact upon which we can rest rights claims. Theorists thus far have falsely equated the moral-ontological status of privacy and autonomy with their factual-ontological status.

Within the moral ontology of natural rights, and as aspects of our conception of human beings as dignified, privacy and autonomy are inversely identical given that the first provides passive and the second active dignity. The factual ontology, however, which is the only one theorists thus far have assumed to exist, does not initially include a conception of dignity within which privacy and autonomy might be seen as inversely identical. Indeed, besides physical properties, privacy and autonomy are, at this level, the only entities available for comparison. Sensing, then, what they have failed to analyze, that these properties do bear an inverse relationship morally, thinkers are left to assume that one is the "negative" version of the other, rather than that they are two aspects of the way we conceive of people morally. They assume a pre-moral status for a certain identity between privacy and autonomy that in fact comes to be only through and within the moral-metaphorical representation of these properties. They have not analyzed closely enough the structure of rights or the metaphysics of morality.

As a result of this failing, such theorists can defend a claim that privacy falls under freedom as "negative freedom."Perhaps because there has historically been more philosophical interest in "freedom," they choose to reduce privacy rather than autonomy. It is not clear, however, that on this view freedom should not be construed as being simply positive or active privacy whereby we claim the right to act in the world without having our motives, in a sense, scrutinized by others. Freedom would then be seen as a kind of privacy of action as compared with the more passive, and infinitely larger, privacy of thought. Perhaps we could even construe freedom as "negative privacy," being "concealment from" the valid scrutiny by others of fully discernible acts.Or perhaps privacy and autonomy are not identical in the way that "negative freedom" theories might suggest.

Clark, expressing the negative freedom view, rejects the potential of metaphysics to ground morality[26] and claims that "nothing is by nature private."[27] Nonetheless, she wants to make claims about the "being" of privacy and freedom. What is in fact an ontological identity between the two – as psychological natural properties that instigate the factual ontology of natural rights – she takes to be a kind of definitional identity. Two things that have equal being are taken by her to be therefore the same thing. As quoted above, she tells us that because "one must be private to be free and be free to be private," privacy and freedom are therefore identical; at the very least, "the one certainly entails the other."

What Clark does not see is that privacy and freedom "entail" one another because they exist in the same way, as impenetrable elements of the human psyche, and not because they are definitionally identical (a notion whose rejection she implicitly admits is possible). We cannot have privacy without freedom because neither is ontologically prior to the other as an aspect of human nature. To explain more fully, let me add that we cannot have privacy or freedom, one without the other; *or* without also requiring food to live. All three of these exist as facts about humans. Privacy and autonomy, however, are unique in that once they become rights, on the basis of their status as facts, they cannot be fully violated. In this sense they are ontologically inseparable.

Hence the error of the "negative freedom" theorists stems from their failure to distinguish the ontology of fact from the ontology of value. For though we do unify privacy and autonomy within a metaphor of human dignity as two aspects of the same moral conception of human beings, we do not thereby make privacy and autonomy identical to one another by equating them with "dignity," much less freedom. Rather, we arrive at a metaphor that reflects the factual-ontological sameness of (innate) privacy and autonomy by representing both.

Some degree of definitional sameness may seem to emerge from metaphorical unification through a word because the same word – dignity – can be used in explaining our rights to both privacy and autonomy. The conception of these two elements of humanity as identical themselves, however, cannot be achieved through this metaphor because while they can both be evoked in explaining our conception of humans as dignified, the converse is not true. "Human dignity" can be used to explain our rights to privacy and autonomy only, and not to explain privacy and autonomy in themselves. Remember that the conception of humans as dignified, while ontologically prior to the value we place on privacy and autonomy, is nonetheless subsequent to innate privacy and autonomy.

Recognition of the unification of innate privacy and autonomy as inversely identical within our conception of persons as dignified deepens our sense of how that conception represents metaphorically the ontological status of privacy and autonomy as innate. While the notion (discussed in chapter 1) that human dignity is innate functions also to represent the innateness of privacy and autonomy, the unification of the latter within the concept of human dignity clarifies this innateness as signifying ontological equivalence. The need for food is just as "innate" as original privacy and autonomy, but it does not inhere within us in the same way. So while the need for food takes its "being" from the same factual-ontological level as psychological natural properties, it nonetheless is not ontologically equivalent to them; it has not the same kind of being.

Hence we have two aspects of the human psyche that, while distinct, are ontologically equivalent to one another. Our innate tendency to acknowledge that equivalence through a metaphorical unification leads many into confusion about the definitional distinctness of privacy and freedom. These two are, however, both innately and pragmatically distinct.

## DISTINGUISHING PRIVACY AND
## AUTONOMY RELATIONALLY

One may object to the arguments above, saying that indeed privacy and autonomy are inversely related through more than the conception of human beings as dignified. In defence of this objection, one may point to any of a number of discussions of specific rights that see privacy and freedom in opposition. An example of such a discussion would be one in which it is recognized that we are "quite right in placing privacy and freedom of speech ... in opposition to one another."[28] Courts and citizens alike recognize that we are entitled to privacy only to the extent that it does not infringe the justifiable freedom of others, and vice versa.

Such an objection, however, forgets whereof it speaks. All talk of the tension between privacy and freedom is talk of bestowed *rights*. It belongs within the context of the post-bestowal rights trade described here as being the first we see of these rights, although it is the product of much that requires analysis. The conception of humans as dignified is already in play at this point, and the tension we feel is that between the dignity of agency (which gives us any of our rights to freedom) and the dignity of self-concealment, the source of our privacy rights. It is interesting at any rate to think of equating two rights – as being both essentially "freedom" – that are distinct at least to the extent that they are sometimes opposed to one another. Negative freedom theorists would argue that this opposition is born of their being "positive" and "negative" forms of the same thing, but an examination of the pre-moral stage of innate privacy and autonomy will demonstrate that this is not the case.

In my earlier discussion of the virtual inviolability of psychological natural rights, I provided my version of Wasserstrom's very useful thought-violation problem: that if there were a "thought-violation machine" that could discern and expose all the contents of a person's mind, it would have to work constantly in order to violate fully a person's privacy. I indicated that innate privacy was protected from ultimate violation by the fact of the autonomous production of the thoughts discerned. My purpose was to demonstrate the ontological location of inviolable privacy and autonomy as co-existing in the "moment" of thought production. Implicit in that passage, however, is a defence also of the notion that innate autonomy has the capacity to "protect," as it were, innate privacy through the fact of autonomous thought production.

Alan Westin's discussion of the relation between privacy and autonomy[29] contains a strong defence of the notion that the "individual's sense that it is he who decides when to 'go public' is a crucial aspect of his feeling of autonomy"[30] and that therefore "the private personality is the … ultimate shield of personal autonomy."[31] Arguing this case, in my view, is somewhat more difficult than arguing that autonomy shields privacy. For what does it matter to autonomy that someone should find a way to observe the pre-articulated production of a thought as long as the thought is indeed produced by the thinker observed? It would seem that while the autonomy of thought production is required to preserve privacy, privacy is not required to preserve autonomy. This view, however, neglects what it would mean fully to violate autonomy.

For though we may reach a new level of privacy violation in observing the autonomous production of thought, we do not violate autonomy.[32] To do so we must remove the capacity of the individual to produce his own thoughts. Yet as long as we do produce our own thoughts, there is still that "moment" of privacy, the privacy of the indecipherability of pre-articulated thinking. That is the privacy that shields autonomy, just as it is shielded by autonomy. While Westin, in seeing the private personality as the ultimate shield of personal autonomy, argues essentially this view of the protection innate privacy affords innate autonomy, he does so only for the macrocosm. He speaks of privacy and autonomy as they function, and help us to function, within the trade that I described at the beginning of this chapter; I speak of the innate, individual privacy and autonomy that determines that function.

SUMMING UP

From my discussion thus far there emerge three distinct ways of viewing the relationship between privacy and autonomy. We most commonly see privacy and autonomy as related through conflict within the rights trade of post-bestowal society. We see them as rights in conflict. The conflict of one person's privacy with another's freedom is thought by many theorists to show that privacy is a "negative freedom."This, then, is the second way to see privacy and autonomy as related. Anyone holding this view, however, must admit that privacy and autonomy bear at least the distinctness that comes about through their being inversely related, rather than identical.

A third way to see privacy and autonomy as related is to see them as interdependent, though distinct at all levels at which they function. This view can be understood through examination of the relation of privacy and autonomy within the conception of human beings as dignified. I hold that while privacy is represented as the dignity of self-concealment, autonomy is represented as the dignity of agency. Unlike other theorists, however, who connect these two entities through dignity, I have suggested that human dignity is not factually innate but rather enters the ontology of rights after original privacy and autonomy while being nonetheless morally original.

I have shown that the common view of human dignity as factually innate arguably supports the negative freedom view of privacy. For if dignity is a factually innate human property, and if privacy and autonomy are both parts of dignity at that level of existence, then privacy and autonomy are innately, actually the same – they are both "dignity." Of course, proponents of the negative freedom view argue that they are both "freedom." What they can borrow from the common dignity theorists is a conception of privacy and autonomy as definitionally, as well as ontologically, the same. It is a short step from there to accommodating the apparent opposition of privacy and autonomy by conceiving them as inversely definitionally the same.

My theory cannot be borrowed to that end because the sameness-in-dignity provided by my theory is an ontological, rather than a definitional, sameness. I see privacy and autonomy as "the same" in dignity only insofar as our conception of human dignity metaphorically represents their identical ontological status as factually innate. Since I do not hold dignity to be inborn, the fact that privacy and autonomy are two aspects of dignity does not render them two aspects of the same idea.

The third view of the relation between privacy and autonomy – my view – points to a distinction between innate and morally conceived privacy and autonomy and suggests that previous theorists have appreciated the "morally conceived" version only, having failed to analyze how innate properties ground that version. I am not, of course, the first to see certain features, or facts about, people as having both a non-moral, empirical sense and a moralized sense. What I reject is any kind of contract theory, sacred or secular, that sees the construction of a moral prescription from a non-moral property as based in anything but a psychologically constructed, intermediary conception of human beings as dignified. I reject both duty to God (sacred self-interest) and duty to survive (secular self-interest) as reasons why we bestow rights.

The psychological natural properties of the pre-moral innate self reveal an interdependence between entities seen as opposed in the other realms. Privacy is (virtually) inviolable in that thought production is always autonomous, and autonomy is so in that thought production is always private. Alan Westin points to the need for privacy, within the trade, in the preservation of autonomy but does not analyze the interdependence of these properties as they exist originally. He says that we must protect privacy to protect autonomy; I say that privacy and autonomy innately protect one another. I do not by this mean to refute Westin but rather to provide the metaphysical (even psychological) underpinnings of his macrocosmic claim, a claim that recognizes interdependence rather than opposition. Like the other ways of viewing the relation between privacy and autonomy, interdependence requires that they be distinct.

### PRACTICE AND THEORY: CONNECTING THE THREE RELATIONS

Before addressing the matter of distinguishing privacy and autonomy definitionally, as opposed to connecting them relationally, let me further elaborate the connection between oppositional and interdependent views of the privacy/autonomy relation by describing society as a macro-organism. Such a view of society will enable us to recreate the interdependence of privacy and autonomy at the macrocosmic level, a level at which they have mistakenly been viewed as oppositional.

Although privacy and autonomy, as individual rights, do indeed come into conflict in the macrocosm of the rights trade, they nonetheless bear an interdependent relationship as macrocosmic *ideals.* Conflict between these entities as rights results from conflict regarding what constitutes preserving human dignity within specific contexts. One person will argue, for example, that human dignity is most abundantly preserved through permitting a reporter's freedom of expression (and society's freedom of information) in publishing a photograph of a politician's unsavoury romp at the beach. His opponent will argue that the transgression of the politician's dignity of concealment, in publishing evidence of a romp entirely unrelated to his political duties, far outweighs the reporter's dignity of agency. None of this means, however, that privacy and freedom are inherently opposed or that one is the inverse of the other.

Indeed, as macrocosmic ideals protected by the moral conception of humans as dignified, these entities function interdependently on the broad scale just as they do within the individual. By the fact that we hold privacy as an ideal, we are certain so to revere autonomy (and vice versa) because these two ideals, as ideals, are ontologically equivalent on the moral scale just as they are equivalent on the factual scale, as properties. One cannot uphold the dignity of human beings without upholding both their privacy and their autonomy (in some way) because these two entities together constitute that broader moral ideal. Hence we find a "unity in diversity" in the macrocosmic interdependence of privacy and autonomy, as ideals, within the very social context where they are sometimes opposed as rights. It is the distinction between the factual and the moral ontologies of natural rights that helps to unravel the mystery of how we could view as inherently opposed (or "inverse") two aspects of people and of cultural ideology that are ontologically equivalent, though definitionally distinct, at both the factual and the moral levels.

This "mystery" can be further resolved through an examination of the metaphor of dignity and how it functions to reflect both the ontological equivalence and the definitional distinctness of innate privacy and autonomy. The unifying metaphor ("of dignity") can easily be taken to represent definitional equivalence rather than the ontological equivalence that it does express because the definitional distinctness of these entities cannot be reflected in one word. In other words, the metaphor of dignity does not serve adequately to express the distinctness of privacy and autonomy. It reflects their ontological sameness and provides a concept around which to posit definitional sameness. Ironically, their definitional distinctness in the face of their moral-ontological unity provides a concept of "diversity in unity."Hence we find "diversity in unity" at the ritual level of bestowal of these rights and "unity in diversity" at the level of the rights trade. Too many have tried to argue "unity only" through the concept of dignity or "diversity only" through the fight for rights. But we must distinguish ontological from definitional "sameness," and factual from moral ontology.

## DISTINGUISHING PRIVACY AND AUTONOMY DEFINITIONALLY

When I speak of the "definitional difference" between privacy and autonomy, I do not refer to a distinction that can be made with reference to a dictionary. Rather, I refer to the matter of what is inherently different about privacy and autonomy at the pre-moral stage. Why are they ontologically equivalent yet not even "inversely" the same thing? Before synthesizing the literature in support of my claim regarding the interdependence of privacy and autonomy, let me make explicit the distinction for which I have been preparing.

At the pre-moral, innate level of the individual, autonomy is the production, by the individual, of his or her own thoughts, while privacy is the inherent concealment, or inaccessibility to others, of that process. However ontologically equivalent or interdependent these properties are, and no matter how unifying the moral-metaphorical conception of that equivalence or that interdependence may be, the production of a thought and the concealment of that act are different. To say, as a negative freedom proponent might, that the inherent concealment of the autonomous production of thought is the freedom from observation, by others, of that process is to play with words and to confuse entities with the relations between them. I could argue, by the same token, that the act of producing one's own thought is the positive act of privacy that protects one from the invasive production of one's thoughts for one by another. It is the essential moment of active, or positive, privacy upon which all other freedoms are based. Both errors of definition – i.e., defining privacy as autonomy, or autonomy as privacy – result from equating ontological equivalence with definitional equivalence or, more accurately, with ontological (essential) "sameness." Privacy is a "freedom from" only at the level of the post-bestowal rights trade and only in the sense that all rights are either "freedoms to" or "freedoms from."

## INTERDEPENDENCE SUPPORTED

Support for my theory of the initially hidden interdependence of privacy and autonomy both as innate properties and as cultural ideals can be found piecemeal in much of the theoretical literature. Of particular interest to me are certain remarks of Arnold Simmel in "Privacy Is Not an Isolated Freedom,"[33] and of Paul A. Freund in "Privacy: One Concept or Many."[34]

Though Simmel rejects the notion that metaphysics need come into play in theoretical discussions of privacy, he nonetheless bases his cross-disciplinary argument in developmental psychology and makes valuable claims about the relationship between individual conceptions of the self and societal conceptions of the individual. He tells us: "Privacy boundaries ... are self boundaries. The self may be an abstract psychological concept or a metaphysical one, but our concern is not with any definition of an abstract concept, but with the social processes that delimit the space of free movement of the individual, which is reflected in the individual's own definition of his self. Conversely, those individual definitions of self collectively become part of the social definition of the individual."[35] While clearly in support of my earlier argument that ideals of personhood originate in individual self-conception, Simmel advances the argument only with respect to Western culture. For he goes on to state that such a relationship obtains only in systems like ours where the individual is ideologically central. The anthropological literature, however,[36] to which Simmel does not refer, makes a strong case for accepting the universality of this relationship in all cultures, especially around the matter of privacy and in spite of any conceptions other cultures may have that individuals exist "for the institutions."[37] The privacy, autonomy, and dignity of the individual need not be seen as unimportant simply because the individual serves some greater purpose or structure. And indeed there is no evidence that such a view is central to any culture, at least not at the level of ritual, rather than trade privacy.

Also useful to the relationship I propound between innate privacy and autonomy and the social ideals of privacy and autonomy is Freund's discussion of interests, rights, principles, and rules, especially as it culminates in a critical discussion of the usefulness of principles of privacy rather than rules of privacy. While Freund's focus is on privacy alone, what he says can be applied also to my discussion of autonomy.

After telling us at the outset that the law, "like other branches of thought, lives by metaphor, moves by simile, and organizes itself by concepts,"[38] Freund embarks first upon an exegetical account of the historical development of privacy and then upon a critique of the concept of privacy that has emerged from that history. In critiquing the concept Freund distinguishes two ways of seeing the right to privacy, one being a reductionist view in which all privacy claims are considered reducible to a subset of distinct legal rights (a view I shall address in chapter 4) and the other being a "unitary" concept.

Against the view of privacy as a unitary concept, Freund raises the matter of privacy's becoming "too greedy a legal concept" given "the disparity of central issues" that fall under its rubric, such as freedom of the press or "the search for truth in the administration of justice."[39] He tells us that privacy, as a legal concept, "might give excessive protection to an interest in human dignity."[40]

On the other hand, we are told, the concept of a right to privacy might be seen as useful "in order to offset an equally large rhetorical counterclaim: freedom of inquiry, the right to know, liberty of the press."[41] Clearly Freund is addressing privacy as it exists within the rights trade as sometimes opposed to autonomy, and though he recognizes its connection to human dignity, he does not see dignity as necessarily fundamental to trade entitlements. Or does he?

Freund continues his discussion by pointing to the value of concepts (ideals?) to "provide, despite the metaphor, a cutting or a growing edge,"[42] a gauge by which to determine the details of the trade. He also points to the significance of the question "whether privacy has a legitimating unity as a social-psychological concept," by which he means that if "we define an interest as a claim, demand, need, or concern, and a right as a legally protected interest, should privacy be accorded the status of a right?"[43] Thus, he looks to the innate needs or concerns (properties) of the individual to discover a source not only for rights but for social ideals.

In answering his question Freund invokes the fundamental psychological importance of privacy to individual flourishing within both intimate and social contexts, to the traditional conception of both the "sacred and the sexual" as inherently private, and to the universality of ideals and norms of privacy across cultures. The one thing he does not provide is an explanation of why privacy emerges as it does (because it is an innate, inviolable property of all persons) and of how it develops from an individual property to an ideologically supported right.

Having established privacy as an interest (something as easily, if not more easily, done for autonomy), Freund considers whether it is "viable as a legal concept [i.e., a right] as well."[44] While my argument goes more along the lines of how it is that we are entitled to privacy, Freund nonetheless provides support for my claims regarding the derivation of rights from ideals, and, indirectly, for my theory of the interdependence of privacy and autonomy even within the rights trade in which they seem to be, in some way, opposed. For Freund ultimately argues that privacy is viable less as a rule of law than as a principle of law. He distinguishes a "rule" as a "particularization" that defines law within specific contexts and prescribes "with precision." A principle, on the other hand, "is a more plastic formulation, useful for predicting and shaping the course of legal development."[45] Privacy, in other words, is viable as an ideal in the sense in which an ideal, like a principle, is overarching, non-specific, and evocative of prescription. Moreover, it is an ideal that grows from the "interests" (properties) of individuals and that stands as a basis for moral prescription at the social level. Given that Freund initially values a unifying concept of privacy for the protection it provides from our ideals of freedom, it is not difficult to see the hidden interdependence, or unity in diversity, of these post-bestowal ideals as ideals. While the protection of both these ideals provides cultures with the "give and take" of seeming opposition, the protection of one only would provide the tyranny of "take" alone.

### PRIVACY ISOLATED

Having revealed the relation between privacy and autonomy as actually interdependent, while apparently opposed, and having also distinguished them within the context of their interdependence, I am now free to isolate privacy from my theory of natural rights as the chief focus of my thinking about natural rights. I have delineated a five-part theory of the structure of rights, beginning with innate properties, which are the "seeds" of these rights within individuals, and concluding with the post-bestowal rights trade. From this point I shall refer sometimes to the "rights trade" and sometimes, where appropriate, to the "privacy trade," which is a subset of the overall trade in rights. Both "trades" refer to a system of claim-making, waiving, and overriding in which claims are legitimated morally on the basis of how directly they can be shown to grow out of either absolute, static norms or the ideal of dignity at the basis of those norms. Both trades establish fluctuating or non-absolute rights (conceivable as manifest-derivative, rather than manifest-symbolic, norms), which are open to scrutiny and alteration on the basis of the same ideals that are said to legitimate them.

Clearly, then, to conceive the right to privacy as the right to be "let alone" is to conceive it too broadly, on the basis of the fluctuating entitlements of the trade, most specifically on the basis of a bestowed right to a private life. Defining the limits of that entitlement is impossible without first knowing the entire history of the trade in rights. Hence the metaphor of the "right to be let alone" has far too vague a referent for it to function adequately as a definition of the right to privacy. Indeed this right is more appropriately described, rather than defined, as a right that evolves within individuals and cultures in the way that I have thus far shown.

# 3 Defending the Ontological Theory

There are three main objections, closely related and potentially subversive, to the theory of the ontological structure of natural rights as the foundation of our right to privacy. According to the first, arguing that bestowed rights are grounded ultimately in innate human properties is to commit the famous "naturalistic fallacy."[1] In answer I remind the reader that obligation towards individual privacy and autonomy is here understood to emerge not directly from facts but rather from a certain ideal of personhood. I shall mitigate the leap from fact to ideal by drawing a distinction between value and prescription.

The second objection demands that I show why my view of personhood should be accepted. It will be seen that many natural rights theorists support the validity of deriving moral obligation from social ideals in general, and from ideals of personhood in particular. Beyond such support, I shall demonstrate that the ideal I put forward is justifiable because it is grounded in psychological research about the nature of human beings. The final objection concerns the universality of the conception of human beings as dignified and the essentialism inherent in such a view. To establish the legitimacy of this assumption, I shall return to the solutions to the first two problems. There are mitigating elements within my theory that allow certain essentialist claims regarding human nature to obtain without their traditional prescriptive force. In addition, the psychological findings of Lawrence Kohlberg bolster the defence of universalism and other aspects of my theory. Finally, the role I claim for the moral conception of human beings as innately dignified will emerge as the pivotal issue in this chapter.

## THE NATURALISTIC FALLACY

As noted, there is a large body of literature supporting my notion of locally absolute manifest-symbolic privacy and autonomy norms and the fluctuating, derivative norms that emerge from them. Charles Fried, for instance, argues forcefully that privacy in general is protected through societally constructed symbolic means.[2] Fried's focus is on the significance of privacy to the intimacy of our most important social relations and on the fact that privacy can be "gravely compromised" in any concrete social system by such things as the rights of others or the enforcement of laws. To the end of protecting privacy, Fried argues, society "designates certain areas, intrinsically no more private than others, as symbolic of the whole institution of privacy, and thus deserving of protection beyond their particular importance."[3]

While Fried's work can be invoked in support of my conception of manifest-symbolic norms, he nonetheless provides a view of the right to privacy as derived only from social necessity or personal necessity within a social context.[4] My theory, however, sees this right, with our autonomy rights, as reflective of both social ideals and innate human facts.

The role I claim, then, for the universal conception of human beings as innately dignified requires careful defence. While I have already defended my conception of the relation that obtains between our natural privacy and autonomy and our view of people as innately dignified,[5] a still more fundamental problem exists for my notion that privacy, with autonomy, is itself a natural human property on the basis of which we can arrive at prescriptions with regard to privacy, autonomy, or dignity. This is the danger of succumbing to the classic charge of Moore and, before him, Hume, that we commit the naturalistic fallacy in attempting to derive an "ought" from an "is."[6]

In my theory, however, obligation is not derived from natural properties but rather is constructed upon a certain moral view of people that is both instigated by and metaphorically representative of a fact about human nature. Hence I do not argue directly from is to ought; instead, I see an intermediary stage in which a fact about human beings (their innate privacy and autonomy) leads to a metaphorical, moral conception of people (as innately dignified), which conception both represents the fact and grounds the construction of the obligation. Our respective rights to privacy and autonomy, then, are constructed only indirectly upon the fact or "natural law" that all people, by virtue of being individuals, possess innately private and autonomous natures. They are so constructed through our attempt to represent innate facts in a moral conception of human beings as innately dignified. This moral conception is the direct source of our construction of prescriptions regarding dignity, autonomy, and privacy. But we should analyze this still more deeply.

It will be remembered from the first chapter that innate facts must first be perceived before they can enter the realm of things "described." Describing innate privacy and autonomy non-metaphorically and non-morally can be done simply by acknowledging the biological fact that "humans are innately private and autonomous." Such a description stands also as a certain kind of non-metaphorical conception of people, as being innately private and autonomous. It might be argued that while I do not view rights themselves as constructed directly upon this descriptive fact, I nonetheless make the leap from "is" to "ought" in making the leap from this non-moral, non-metaphorical conception of human beings to a moral-metaphorical conception of human beings as dignified. It might also be thought that my conception contains a value judgment, however weak. This criticism, which takes the is/ought problem to be a fact-to-value problem, stipulates that it is logically problematic to claim that I bypass the naturalistic fallacy by arguing neither from fact to value, nor from value to value, but rather from intermediary metaphor to value. Here is the objection:

1. If the middle stage is a value judgment, then my conclusion follows but there is a foundational problem.
2. If the middle stage is a statement of fact, then my conclusion does not follow.
3. The middle claim must be either a value judgment or a statement of fact.
4. Either my conclusion does not follow, or my view has a foundational problem.[7]

Clearly, I reject the third premise and do so on the twin basis of a distinction between two senses of the concept of valuing, and of the unique nature of metaphorical description.

Implicit in the third premise is a term, "judgment," which presupposes that any expression, or construction, of value is prescriptive. It presupposes either that to value something is always to prescribe with regard to that something or, at least, that to value something is to "judge" with regard to value. As the first part of a two-part rebuttal of the potential charge against my theory, I now defend a distinction between a non-prescriptive and a prescriptive sense of value. I hold that the conception of human beings as dignified, because it is a descriptive metaphor, is a non-prescriptive value: a value, in other words, that contains no implicit judgment.

The notion of "value judgment," in the third premise of the argument above, can be taken in two ways. First, it can be taken to refer to a judgment we make that innate privacy and autonomy are morally valuable. It can also be taken to refer to a judgment we make about moral values, that they all entail duties. I reject both these possibilities.

The moral conception of people as dignified does not constitute a judgment we make that innate privacy and autonomy are morally valuable. The construction of a descriptive metaphor of innate properties is not a derivation of value from fact. It is a moral picture, as it were, that adds value to the properties it describes (albeit on the basis of a desire that these properties be valued) but that cannot possibly constitute a judgment of the value of those properties.

As a metaphorical construction, then, our conception of human beings as dignified is not a derivation. Though our innate privacy and autonomy mean to us that we are (metaphorically) innately dignified, that meaning is not taken from those properties, it is constructed through moral description. The term "description" may suggest that what we construct is indeed a picture of what inheres in innate properties, except that the status of that description as metaphorical defers the necessity of ascribing innate value to the properties described. As metaphor, the moral description of innate privacy and autonomy adds to the properties described, creating more of an interpretive than a realist picture.[8] What is "added" is moral value, given that we are not born with dignity. Hence we do not judge innate properties to have positive moral value and then, on that basis, derive a conception of human dignity. Rather, we construct an interpretation of innate properties that employs moral metaphor to add to those properties the value we wish they had innately. The value we construct is inherent, once constructed, but not innate.

I turn now to the second sense in which my intermediary human dignity might be construed as a moral judgment, i.e., as a judgment we make that duties are owed innate privacy and autonomy because they evoke the construction of a moral conception of human dignity. Many theorists believe that a certain moral conception of people necessitates the right-bearing status of human beings. They believe that if the conception is acceptable, then prescriptions regarding it follow logically. I do not hold this view of the construction of rights. I conceive of a distinction between the non-problem of the move from fact to (non-prescriptive) value and the potential problem of the leap from value (so conceived) to prescription. To emphasize further the non-prescriptive nature of human dignity at the moral-metaphorical level, let me remind the reader that while the metaphor of dignity does not constitute a judgment about the value of innate privacy and autonomy, it does constitute a metaphorical reconstruction of the value of virtually inviolable properties. While this construction adds value, then, to innate properties, it is absurd to think of it as a construction that, in itself, entails obligation to those properties: it metaphorically represents the inviolable. While I have argued throughout that dignity can indeed be transgressed, I have made it clear that transgression is made possible by the construction of static norms. Such norms do not exist at the moral-metaphorical level; they are constructed upon it to form the manifest-symbolic level of the structure of rights. I conceive a distinction between valuing what is inviolable and constructing duties to symbolize that value. I shall address the value-to-prescription problem at a later point.

To sum up, the intermediary conception of human dignity is not a value judgment in either of the two senses in which it could be so construed. It is, rather, a value construction that adds value to, rather than derives it from, the properties it metaphorically represents. Moreover, it is a simple non-prescriptive value, representing, as it does, properties that are inviolable. So my conception of human dignity as a distinctly metaphorical construction defers the naturalistic fallacy charge for the matter of moving from fact to value. It defers that charge to the point at which I move from simple value to prescriptive value. The problematic "leap" for my theory occurs in the transition from the moral-metaphorical to the manifest-symbolic stage – though as we shall see, metaphor and symbolism also defer the fallacy.

## ON DERIVING NATURAL RIGHTS FROM MORAL CONCEPTIONS OF PERSONHOOD

I have answered potential fallacy charges by saying that I do not espouse the derivation of values directly from facts. Hence I must justify, in the face of my naturalism, the view that obligation is constructed upon moral ideals, or metaphors of personhood. In this we come to the reason for my claim that natural rights are originally created, as being constructed upon innate properties of people, but societally bestowed, as being constructed from a metaphor of human dignity. In defending and elaborating this aspect of my theory, I will evoke the work of previous proponents of natural rights who have espoused natural rights, either explicitly or implicitly, while deriving human obligation towards them from ideals rather than from factual properties. I engage them to support my own theory as well as to reject the notion that obligation is logically entailed by an acceptable moral conception of human beings. Let us turn briefly to the early history of natural law and natural rights.

### Hugo Grotius and the Problem of Obligation

Grotius, who is accepted as the "founder" of the modern school of natural law, has had far too great an influence on the history of political thought to receive comprehensive treatment here. It is important, however, that I address two specific aspects of his work, especially as they are analyzed by Knud Haakonssen in "Hugo Grotius and the History of Political Thought."[9] There is a discrepancy between the implications of Grotius's view of natural rights and his view that indeed there is a law of nature, human obligation to which "could only be seen to stem from God."[10] Bearing that in mind, I shall address his view of natural rights.

Haakonssen tells us that "Grotius's most important contribution to modern thought was his theory of rights,"[11] especially insofar as it paves the way to seeing the law of nature as having both "a validity independent of God's will"[12] and an obligatory force that is independent of that validity. Moreover, though Grotius himself failed to see it, his theory of rights not only distinguishes "the validity of the content of natural law ... [from] the obligation to keep natural law,"[13] it does so in a move that also eliminates the need for either natural law or obligation thereto.

Before describing just how Grotius's theory of rights achieves these ends, it is necessary to clarify the problem of obligation as it existed for natural law theorists of the seventeenth and eighteenth centuries, and as I conceive of it. Before Grotius, Francisco Suarez (1548–1617) had also "made explicit the distinction between the content of the law of nature and its obligation,"[14] showing that "rational insight into the goods of life which are man's natural aims"[15] cannot, in itself, make the law that is the object of that insight obligatory. While Suarez's theory defined the will of a superior God as the source of obligation to natural law, and while Grotius himself claimed God as that source, Grotius nonetheless developed a theory of natural rights that implies, initially, that obligation to natural law could obtain even without God. For contemporary natural rights theorists such as myself, this provides a hopeful starting point.

Haakonssen tells us that Grotius's most important innovation in developing his theory of natural rights was to view *ius* (the just) as something that a person *has* rather than as "something that an action or state of affairs ... *is* when it is in accordance with [natural] law."[16] The concept is thus "subjectivized," as a power or a "moral quality" of the person, rather than being an "objective condition appointed by law."[17] The obvious implication of this view is that it opens "the idea of human life as the exercise of competing individual rights."[18] It does this by rendering "justice" a matter for debate. Grotius formulates it somewhat differently, suggesting that the social life to which we are bound by nature is "simply the respecting of one another's rights, subjectively conceived."[19] Grotius did not see the implication that since "the rational insight into the [validity of the content of natural law] consists in no more than the common ability to exercise our individual rights as ... required by the ordinary circumstances of human life, there is ... really no need for natural law and thus for an obligation to natural law, whether of divine or other origin."[20]

Grotius provides, then, the all-important conception of obligation to the "natural" without divine reference and a conception of rights as originating within individuals. The latter feature is of particular importance to the support of my own theory, while the former is important to any contemporary theory of rights that does not view rights as entirely constructed. Not provided by Grotius, however, is a view of rights as inhering in people in a pre-moral sense, as properties without obligation attached to them. Instead, he sees rights themselves as innate and, in that, provides a foundation for contemporary theories unlike my own in which natural rights are seen to be defensible only on grounds that they inhere in people complete with obligation, such that obligation is ontologically equivalent to the innate qualities in which it inheres. Such views ignore the possibility of a dual ontology of natural rights with its morality of metaphor, preferring to see morality as innate in the same way that such properties as privacy, autonomy, and the need for food are innate. While I have already defended the ontological distinction between psychological and physical properties, I must object to these theories on further grounds, to follow.

Grotius's theory provides a conception of moral personhood, while my theory provides a moral conception of personhood. This distinction is significant because understanding it will clarify, for Grotius's view, a problem that might seem to be unique to my own of how it is that we can derive obligation from a non-original moral "way of conceiving" of people that does not require that people be innately moral. Were we originally moral, as Grotius claims we are, the obligation of others towards our moral propensities and rights would be given, as would our obligation to theirs. I submit, however, that Grotius merely skips the description of a step in the ontology of natural rights and so sees a way of conceiving of people as indeed the way that people are. In doing this he does not eliminate the problem of deriving obligation from ideals; he merely ignores the problem, preferring to incorporate those ideals into his conception of original personhood.

For what is any "conception of moral personhood" if not a moral way of representing certain perceived facts about human beings? Someone might object that indeed what is perceived is a moral nature; but that person would be hard-pressed to describe this perceived nature in terms irreducible to matters of instinct or of physical and psychological natural properties. For instance, an individual's concern for others need not be seen as reflecting that person's factually innate moral nature. Such concern can arguably be reduced to reproductive and parenting instincts, or to some other survival-based instincts. An individual's concern with rights can arguably be reduced to his or her perception of physical and psychological natural properties. Such properties are the seeds of our morality but not the seat of our morality; an argument must be made to get from the fact of such properties to rights regarding them. Without revelation to guide us, we have only our own thinking about our own natures. A minimalist view of moral personhood, on the other hand, that sees people as moral beings simply because we make moral judgments, is insufficient to ground a view that we are moral in a way that entitles us to anything.

The objection might be made that the inevitability of the moral-metaphorical construction of rights upon properties renders us virtually innately moral. We must remember, however, that the metaphorical innateness of our moral natures is not ontologically equivalent to the inherent properties whose ontological innateness it represents. The innate moral personhood that Grotius and other natural rights theorists espouse is actually built upon innate properties and tendencies. It is a metaphorical label, a way to conceive what they see.

In showing that Grotius also derives obligation from a conception of personhood, and a conception of personhood from innate properties, I do not, of course, solve my problem; I simply drag another down with me. My purpose, however, is ultimately to distinguish my view from the views of those who see a moral conception of people as constituting a factually innate property of human beings. I recognize the potential vulnerability of my view to the naturalistic fallacy charge, while they suppose that the problem does not exist, given innate moral nature. Grotius simply ignores his leap from fact to value, a leap that I do not see as constitutive of the naturalistic fallacy. In ignoring it, however, he ignores also the leap from fact to prescription.

### A.I. Melden on Deriving Obligation from Ideals of Personhood

A.I. Melden, a contemporary natural rights theorist, also sees moral nature as given in birth. His theory supports mine and exemplifies my claim that we are wrong to ignore the distinction between simple value and prescriptive value in characterizing the "is/ought" problem as a fact-to-value problem. Melden's well-conceived and insightful theory lacks an important description of how life's being innately "moral" necessitates the right-bearing capacity of human beings. It lacks, therefore, not so much a justification for the move from fact to value as a justification for the leap from fact to prescription. Because I do not argue the innateness of our status as moral beings, I do not make this leap.

In the introduction to *Rights and Persons*[21] Melden expresses his goal of contributing to the "revival of interest in the doctrine of human [or natural] rights,"[22] saying that such a conception of rights is quite viable when "stripped … of the absurd idea that such rights may be exercised and accorded under any and all circumstances and without reference to any sort of rational constraints."[23] In the bulk of his book, he discusses rights both as grounds of action and as moral concepts, a discussion that lays the foundation for the sixth chapter, in which he delineates a theory of "Human Rights."[24] Like Grotius, Melden espouses a view of rights that sees morality as original in the same sense in which I see privacy, autonomy, and the need for food as original. Thus he does not address the reducibility of perceived human moral nature and skirts the issue of the naturalistic fallacy, the validity of which he wishes to reject. He nevertheless provides much that is useful to my argument.

Melden puts forward a theory of rights as derivable from a particular conception of personhood. He also addresses the problem of committing the naturalistic fallacy in arguing from facts about people to prescriptions about those facts. He raises the issue by questioning the validity of the fallacy itself, asking, "Is there a set of characteristics constitutive of personhood such that the possession of rights follows logically from the possession of at least some of these characteristics?"[25] In formulating the fallacy in terms of a leap from characteristics to rights, Melden addresses the fact-to-prescription problem rather than the value-to-prescription problem that I must eventually address. First, I will compare and contrast our respective theories both to glean what is useful and to help situate my view.

Fortunately, the assertion of human dignity through the assertion of rights is the very point upon which Melden's conception of humans as right bearers turns. He first rejects various conceptions of human beings – including those that see us as autonomous, having intrinsic worth, rational, or simply capable of feeling pleasure and pain – as not having the capacity to necessitate human rights, for various reasons. He then provides a communitarian argument which holds that the potential for grounding rights in "some sort of attribute that constitutes the essence of human beings ... their rationality, autonomy, uniqueness," is limited by the fact that such references "pertain to their endowments merely as individuals"[26] rather than as members of a moral community. He ultimately resolves the matter of just what supports our status as right bearers by listing a series of fundamental human activities and relationships that are included in that on which "the rights of humans must come to rest ... this enormously complicated and moral form of human life itself."[27]

I have argued that our natural rights are grounded in a specific essentialist attribute of individuals: the universal tendency to conceive of ourselves as innately dignified, which is constructed upon our innate privacy and autonomy. These innate properties are the sort of properties Melden rejects as being insufficient to ground rights. I have also argued that the tendency to conceive of people this way is unique among individual attributes in that it provides a conception of people upon which to construct manifest-symbolic dignity norms. The status I afford such norms as both symbol and manifestation parallels strikingly the role of dignity in Melden's conception of what makes people right bearers. Though he provides no explanation of the source, either within individuals or within communities, of our reverence for dignity, he nonetheless sees the defending of one's human rights (hence of one's dignity) as an assertion (or manifestation) of one's right-bearing status, which also shows (or symbolizes to) others that we are "moral agents on terms of equality with others as members of the moral community."[28] The moral conception of human beings as dignified, then, and the static norms of its manifest-symbolic reconstruction, function in Melden's theory of rights as they do in mine, though not in precisely the same way; for Melden sees the conception of human dignity itself as including manifest-symbolic dignity. He does so because he considers that rights are given in birth.

While we both see human dignity as linking the self to the community, Melden sees the symbolic function of dignity as being simply to demonstrate membership in the moral community and says: "What we label the dignity of a person is not a matter pertaining to some precious internal quality of his – his rationality or autonomy – but that sense he displays of his own status as a being who is authorized by his rights to conduct himself in the expectation that his rights will be honored by others."[29] So rights, to Melden, are born of community and prior to the dignity of their assertion. He provides no clear explanation of the source of one's "sense" of moral status; even if we conceive it as a self-respect learned through seeing the ideals of the community, he provides no clear explanation of the source of those ideals. If they are simply part of the innate moral natures of people born into communities, then we still lack an adequate explanation of those natures, or of the moral nature of community. My view, which sees the moral as constructed upon a rational, if potentially subconscious, process of being, perceiving, and conceiving, better accounts for our sense of ourselves as indeed bearing "precious internal qualities," which qualities define our moral natures sometimes in spite of rather than because of community. By my view, human dignity links these internal qualities to the community in a way that instigates the moral status of these qualities and demands that they be given the manifestation within the community that they have within the individual.

Melden's communitarian view of rights, as I have explicated it thus far, may seem circular since he claims that it is in asserting our rights that we manifestly claim our status as right bearers, a status that is ours due to membership in the human community. We become right-bearers, then, by asserting rights that, paradoxically, we already have. In this rests our dignity, a dignity that our innate rights require us to maintain. This characterization of his theory is somewhat unfair.

Melden sees the same human rights as bearing two different modes of description, if not of being, in the fact that we are born with a set of arguably dormant rights the manifest assertion of which, and only the manifest assertion of which, provides our status both as right bearers of active rights, and as bearers of dignity. Through this distinction between dormant and active rights he avoids the circularity his argument may seem, at first, to have. His view is similar to mine, though what I claim is "dormant" about the first-level being of human rights is the very obligation of others to respect innate properties as indicative of rights; what is dormant for Melden is the right bearer's explicit status as moral being. For him, the right bearer is "born" and has a kind of "coming out," while for me the right bearer is made, albeit with some degree of necessity. The difference turns on our respective views of the nature and function of the conception of humans as dignified. I believe that Melden's view of "dignity" is too simple because he does not explore where it comes from. Indeed, he seems to see dignity as a symbol of our rights rather than rights as symbols of our dignity.

But how could the "enormously complicated and moral form of human life" necessitate the right-holding capacities of human beings without first evoking a conception of what it is for people to have moral access to rights? While moral personhood includes all of the activities and relationships upon which Melden bases our status as right bearers, none of these activities, whether separately or in combination with other activities, makes the leap from the fact of being moral people to the fact of having rights; too much is assumed, and therefore goes unexplained, in the stipulation that we are innately moral. One cannot say that our moral natures give us rights without saying what *is* moral in the nature that gives us rights. But Melden views dignity simply as a performative: in asserting rights one maintains dignity, and this dignity gives us our rights. Ironically, dignity viewed as the conception of personhood that it is catapults us to the right to rights that cannot be ours simply through individual assertion. How it does so I shall presently explain, when I reformulate the naturalistic fallacy as it threatens my theory.

To view the assertion of rights as a performative act that both creates and expresses our dignity as members of the moral community is nevertheless very close to grounding our rights in our dignity. Melden's eagerness to avoid potentially exclusivist ideals as well as the grounding of our rights in specific aspects of ourselves leads him to refuse to make explicit that it *is* human dignity upon which we construct obligation to our innate properties. It is not, however, the practical dignity of assertions that so functions but rather our prior acceptance of a conception of human beings as dignified. For community requires some degree of ideological agreement in order to recognize entitlement; such agreement is not something with which we are born. The conception of people as dignified is an ideal but not an exclusivist one. It represents "precious internal qualities" but is not one itself; it is the name we have given our reverence for the innate desires – or pre-normative natural properties – of individuals. In its status as a universal ideal that is born of innate natural properties, this conception of human dignity is the obvious go-between for ourselves and our communities, not because it allows us to assert what community has already granted us but because it allows community to grant us what we, as individuals, have by nature.

### Summing Up the Distinction

To clarify the distinction between Melden's view and mine, let me reiterate that Melden sees moral community as a necessary and primary fact of human life. In using the word "primary," here as above, I refer to the fact that Melden would view our private and autonomous natures, even in their most basic manifestations as non-transgressible properties, as aspects of an innate moral nature that includes entitlement or obligation at its most basic level. Further to this he views community, viz. moral community, as the source of these innately moral natures. To Melden, being born into moral community makes us the innately moral people we are. On this he bases our right to rights and rejects the naturalistic fallacy by representing the "ought" as a primary fact about humans that need not be derived. Though I recognize that we are often integrated into and to a degree shaped by communities, I think that we more fundamentally struggle to individuate ourselves from our context, and that we view ourselves, at first glance, not as parts of a whole but as individual entities of primary concern. I am an individualist, where Melden is a communitarian. I am not, however, an absolute individualist with regard to entitlement to live according to our innate desires and properties; for I see community as a bestower of entitlement, a "bestowal" that is based not on innate facts but on a human tendency to conceive of people as innately dignified. The moral, in my view, is born of the natural but is a secondary, rather than a primary, natural fact.

The most critical distinction between Melden's view and mine is the distinction between the role we see for human dignity and the significance that distinction has for our respective views of human morality. This distinction also contains the reason why my view is more complete than Melden's, explaining, as it does, more about the moral world.

In viewing the moral world as something given, ultimately, in birth, and human dignity as a given that is repeatedly renewed through assertions of rights, Melden ignores a function of the moral conception of humans as dignified that is the basis of its relevance to morality. In thinking ourselves dignified, in being right-bearers, in asserting rights at all, we give meaning to ourselves and to our lives. It is through this desire for meaning, in conjunction with our capacity for metaphor, that we come to construct a view of ourselves as dignified or even as moral in the first place. The whole metaphorical system of morality is one that evolves from our perception of innate facts about ourselves through our desire to find meaning in these facts. Melden, like Grotius and other innate-human-rights theorists, inadvertently equates the desire for meaning with a fact of meaning and so subsumes the most general metaphorical expression of our lives as meaningful – a notion that we are moral beings – into the "original" stage of his moral world-view. Thus, obligation in Melden's view, like Grotius's, is derived from a moral conception of people, one that sees people not as specifically dignified but, more generally and less informatively, as indeed moral. He fails to recognize the metaphorical nature of the moral view of human beings.

## COMPLETING THE DEFENCE

I have argued that to conceive the "is/ought" problem as a fact-to-value problem wrongly equates prescriptive norms ("oughts") with value norms, which, though normative, are not judgments or prescriptions. I have said that though my conception of human dignity may be a value, it is not a value judgment. Rather, it is a moral-metaphorical description of innate, non-moral facts to which it adds value. Part of what makes it a "simple" value, rather than a prescriptive judgment, is the very universality that also makes it acceptable as an ideal of personhood on the basis of which to construct rights.

The universality to which I refer is the universality of people's theoretical potential to hold this value. I am not arguing that because everyone does it it is an acceptable conception, any more than I would claim that everyone's making a particular judgment makes it any less a judgment. Rather, I argue that everyone has the theoretical potential to arrive at this conception because it is the only possible conception of people at which to arrive on the basis of perceived innate facts. It is not a judgment about these facts because, as a metaphor, it adds to the properties it describes. As a specifically moral metaphor, it adds value to those properties. Clearly, I need to prove the universality of arriving at such a conception of personhood. Unlike many of my predecessors in the field of natural rights, I shall prove this not on the basis of what we can and cannot imagine but rather on the basis of psychological research into the facts of human moral development. Before engaging this research, however, I shall complete my defence against the naturalistic fallacy charge.

As I noted earlier, it is generally accepted that once a conception of personhood is legitimated as accurate and therefore as capable of grounding rights, the naturalistic fallacy is no longer an issue. The argument, at that point, proceeds from value to prescription, rather than from fact to prescription. Yet, as I have argued, many before me have held all value to be prescriptively normative – a view that I deny. Hence I must defend my leap from descriptive value to prescription, rather than from fact to prescriptive value.

I defend this leap on the basis of the function of metaphor and of symbol in my theory. Just as our conception of human beings as dignified is primarily a reconstruction of innate facts that adds value to these facts, so are static norms reconstructions of the metaphor of dignity that describe, or "mean," that metaphor in concrete symbolic terms. While the symbol would indeed seem to "describe" the metaphor as prescriptive, I hold that prescriptiveness is added to the metaphor at the manifest-symbolic level, just as value is added to innate facts at the moral-metaphorical level. I distinguish, then, our desire that innate privacy and autonomy should bear value from the construction of that value in dignity, and our desire that dignity should necessitate obligation from the construction of that obligation in manifest-symbolic norms. Prescription is added, at this level, by the fact that trangressibility is introduced into a concept of dignity as inviolable. Transgressibility is introduced by the concreteness of the symbolic reconstruction of dignity into static norms protecting our bodies, or our tangible selves.

The reader may object that metaphors "add" to language, or description, in ways that symbols do not. Indeed, symbols are thought to mean more than their immediate content, rather than to add qualities to their referends. I do not claim, however, that manifest-symbolic norms add prescriptive value to the conception of human beings as dignified only because they are symbols. Rather, they add that value because they are concrete, or manifest, symbols. These norms symbolize a metaphor. The moral value inherent in the metaphor is symbolized concretely as prescriptive value; it is the value of action, or of the tangible.

In its status as a manifest symbolic reconstruction of dignity, then, the manifest-symbolic construction of prescription defers the problem of the fallacy just as the metaphorical nature of the conception of human beings as dignified defers it for the previous level. For in reconstructing dignity as a manifest symbol, we again add to the entity reconstructed (in this case, human dignity) the prescriptive value we wish it had innately. In my theory, that value is the prescriptive value that protects the transgressible. The body as symbol of transgressibility is the means by which we add prescriptive value where there was none. Prescriptive value cannot be said to have been derived from, in the sense of having been implicit in, human dignity at the moral-metaphorical stage.

If we consider my claim that we universally construct rights in this way, the argument begins to evoke the problem of free will in a pre-determined universe; how do we construct morality if the morality to be constructed is necessarily of a certain content? Yet just as a judgment is no less a judgment for everyone's making it, so a construction is no less a construction for being based on a blueprint. That there are those who do not hold a conception of people as dignified will later be seen as a function of circumstance.

It remains to demonstrate that we all reason, morally, towards a conception of human beings as dignified. So I turn to Lawrence Kohlberg's research on human moral development.

### Engaging Universalist Essentialism

Evident in my brief critique of Melden's view of moral personhood is a general critique of all theories that see moral personhood, and therefore right-bearing capacity, as given inherently in birth. In my view, though our capacity to be moral beings is given in human birth, the ontological facts with which we as individuals are born do not include a moral status as right bearers. The difference between my view of human birth and Melden's is partly the difference between an individualist and a communitarian view.

Implicit in Melden's view is a sort of general essentialism regarding human moral nature that sees all humans as innately right-bearing beings. I escape this initial essentialism because in my view we are only potentially "moral" at birth and not at all right bearing. But I fall prey to a more specific charge of essentialism in claiming that all individuals conceive their innate privacy and autonomy as grounds for their dignity and that such a conception of human dignity is universally the basis of moral personhood and of right-bearing status.

Some might argue that I fall prey to unacceptable essentialism in claiming the inherent privacy and autonomy of all human beings, but I think that this particular charge is quite easily discharged. It would be very difficult to deny the extremely small conceptions I put forward of inherent, inviolable privacy and autonomy as being the concealment and agency of the very thought-production that goes on inside our heads. Moreover, whatever (easily provable) essentialism is entailed by this view is also easily mitigated by the fact that I attach no prescriptive power to those innate properties themselves, seeing obligation rather as constructed upon a moral metaphor for essential human properties. Without prescriptive power, essentialist claims lose much of their power to harm, especially when they refer to all people, rather than just to a particular human subset. Hence the universal essentialist claim that is truly problematic for my theory is the claim that all individuals construct a moral metaphor for their innate privacy and autonomy, and that this metaphor is the conception of humans as innately dignified. For while this metaphor is arguably not in itself prescriptive, it is the basis upon which prescription is constructed, and it is the core concept in my theory of rights.

### Kohlberg and the Problem of Universalism

Lawrence Kohlberg's interdisciplinary approach to the study of morality and of moral education seems to me the most viable approach to an aspect of human living that touches all areas of our lives. Hence I shall draw upon his discussion of the philosophy and psychology of moral development as it appears in the first two volumes of *Essays on Moral Development*.[30] Particularly useful to me in addressing the essentialist problem at hand is Kohlberg's defence of the universalism inherent in his theory of the six stages of justice reasoning. The situation of the conception of humans as

dignified within his theory is also useful. Of interest for my earlier discussion of the naturalistic fallacy and of deriving obligation from conceptions of personhood is Kohlberg's discussion of
the "psychologist's fallacy." First, however, I shall address this
problem of universalist essentialism.

In the preface to *Essays on Moral Development,* Kohlberg tells us
that his research has demonstrated what Socrates, Kant, and
Piaget before him had claimed, that "the first virtue of a person,
school, or society is justice – interpreted in a democratic way as
equity or equal respect for all people."[31] He tells us that this
conception of democratic justice is an answer to "the ontological
question, What are the rights of people, and what duties do these
rights entail?"[32] So we know from the outset that there is a central
place for a conception of humans as dignified, insofar as they are
deserving of respect, within Kohlberg's theory.

When we turn to his delineation of the six moral stages, within
three major levels of justice reasoning, we find a very strong case
not only in support of the existence of a conception of human dignity in all human beings but also in support of my notions that
this dignity is not factually innate and that it is the starting point
of moral obligation.

Kohlberg identifies three major levels of justice reasoning, each
containing two stages. A person who reasons at the first level is
a "pre-conventional person," usually under nine years old, "for
whom rules and social expectations are something external to the
self,"[33] but who, I must add, nonetheless possesses the innate privacy, autonomy, and physical natural properties that I have identified. Most adolescents and adults reason at the second level, as
"conventional" people, "in whom the self is identified with or has
internalized the rules and expectations of others, especially those
of authorities."[34] These, then, are the majority of people, who accept the conception of human beings as dignified especially as it is
symbolized and manifested in both the static and the fluctuating
norms of their culture. They do not think so much about the ideal
of personhood on the basis of which they make claims as they do
about the claims they are permitted, by convention, to make. They
see what has been bestowed without necessarily seeing why, or
how, it has been bestowed.

The "level three, or post-conventional person," is the type of
individual to whom I refer when I speak of people who perceive
their own innate properties and derive from them an explicit

conception of themselves and, therefore, of all people as inherently dignified. They have "differentiated … [themselves] from the rules and expectations of others and [define … their] values in terms of self-chosen principles."[35] The "social perspective" from which such individuals operate is, in Kohlberg's view, the "prior-to-society" perspective that, though it is an "individual" perspective like the "concrete individual perspective" of first-level reasoners, is unique in that it is "a point of view [that] … can be universal … [being] that of *any rational moral individual.*"[36] This is the social perspective of a reasoner who is aware of the second-level "member-of-society" perspective but who re-evaluates that perspective from the point of view of an *individual* "so that social obligations are defined in ways that can be justified to any moral individual."[37] The individualism inherent in my theory, then, if the observations of Kohlberg and his colleagues are accurate, is one that is crucial to any reasoned view of the moral world and does not require us to spend time alone in a desert prior to engaging with society. It is an individualism of reason rather than of social experience.

Of further importance to my theory is Kohlberg's finding that a commitment to morality in general or to moral principles must precede individual acceptance of social laws and values. The capacity itself, then, to value anything morally must exist before concrete social manifestations of that valuing can be devised and accepted. This supports my depiction of the trajectory of the ontological structure of natural rights. Moreover, given the individual perspective of the third-level reasoner, and the requirement of universalizability across cultures and situations for "acceptable" values, it is easy to see, in Kohlberg's theory, support for the notion that such reasoners look inward to determine those acceptable values. They look inward to properties that they have always had and valued intuitively, and they see those properties naturally, as the source of their self-value and of their respect for (or valuing of) others. Such people are able to hold the laws of their culture up to the principles upon which they are based in order to determine legitimacy; they are further able to hold the principles of their culture up to the principles of themselves in order to determine acceptability. I have argued that such people will accept the basic conception of human beings upon which their cultural morality rests because all people, upon attaining this level of moral reasoning, will conceive of human beings as inherently dignified. And Kohlberg's work supports this claim.

## Human Dignity and Kohlberg's Stage Six

I have identified Kohlberg's work as implying the same problem of universalism that is implied by my theory, but I have not yet addressed the resolution of the problem. This is because I intend first to draw supportive parallels between my theory and Kohlberg's and then to address the problem, in part, as he does. Now I need to show both that Kohlberg's findings support individualism and the ontological structure of natural rights as I view it, and that the conception of humans as dignified is the very conception of people upon which he has found the morality of entitlement to rest.

The sixth and final stage of Kohlberg's model of the development of justice reasoning is admittedly a "hypothetical" stage, given that Kohlberg no longer claims fully to have "empirically defined and philosophically justified"[38] it. This is the stage at which the moral reasoner works from the social perspective of "'the moral point of view,' a point of view which ideally all human beings should take toward one another as free and equal autonomous persons."[39] Kohlberg argues that this stage is fully plausible as the end point of his largely empirical theory of moral development, and that the end point is a necessary part of "defining stages as rational reconstructions of ontogenesis."[40] This ideal moral stage, the crowning achievement of human moral aspiration, is manifested "[both] in explicit statements of the intrinsic worth, dignity, or equality of every human being ... [and] in using the criterion of universalizability,"[41] the use of which expresses the fact that dignity so conceived belongs to all people. Why then is the very moral ideal of human beings as dignified, which appears as the starting point of morality in my ontological theory of rights, nevertheless the end point of moral reasoning development within Kohlberg's psychological theory? This difference lies in the distinction between the psychological and the ontological approaches.

Kohlberg seeks to describe a process of rational, or reasoned, morality. He shows how human thinking about morality changes and develops with other aspects of human rationality. He does so through extensive empirical research, which shows that at least the first five stages (and all three levels) of justice reasoning are achievable universally by human beings according to their particular developmental capacities and regardless of their cultural affiliations or differences. Kohlberg describes the process by which many of us move from being egocentric "desirers" to being people who evaluate those desires. We recognize that others have the same desires and recognize both the egocentric need and the social need of their fulfilment. Finally, we evaluate what those desires and the social need of their fulfilment means about people, that they are inherently dignified and equal. He speaks of a rational empirical process that only a few need complete in order to establish a conception of human dignity as a social and individual ideal *even* for people who have not reasoned this far themselves. I shall return to this.

It is not my goal to prove a theory like Kohlberg's but rather to draw on that theory in depicting the world of natural moral entitlement. In my theory, as in Kohlberg's, the human dignity that six-year-olds cannot claim rationally might be claimed irrationally. Yet six-year-olds do so on the basis of a sense they have of their own intrinsic importance, a sense they express through various claims to agency and, I think, to privacy. That six-year olds, however, cannot yet claim their "dignity" is a function of their not yet having constructed that dignity. They have not yet sought the meaning of their desires for agency and privacy or, for that matter, for food and shelter. Others have, however, and children may. If they do, they will come (with age) to Kohlberg's sixth stage, the way of thinking that provides the moral ideal upon which entitlement is based. At the sixth stage we think in a certain moral way about ourselves and others, and in so doing we arrive, universally, at a moral conception of human beings as dignified. Though this dignity is not itself innate, our constructing it is, on Kohlberg's empirically developed theory, inevitable in certain circumstances. Kohlberg, then, provides support for my claim that all people come to think of human beings as dignified, in accordance with their respective rational capacities, but that this "dignity" is innate in us only as a way of conceiving of ourselves. His empirical theory of the rational construction of morality, then, supports my ontological theory through showing that what is the beginning of the moral ontology is indeed not given in birth but is, rather, a way of thinking that we achieve.

The question now arises why it is not necessary that all individuals engage in the rational construction of dignity in order for society to accept the ideal of dignity and to bestow rights accordingly. This is because all people bear the innate psychological natural properties that lead to this ideal, meaning that most, if not all, "conventional" and many "pre-conventional" individuals will derive a strong sense of their own dignity from the combination of their bearing these properties and society's having built norms around the ideal of dignity. Kohlberg's model of the "Phases of Collective Norms"[42] shows that collective norms are first proposed by individuals for group acceptance and that they subsequently go through six more stages involving, first, the acceptance of the norm as an ideal with no duty, or "expectation," attached to it; second, acceptance of the norm with loose expectation attached to it; and finally, acceptance of the norm with attendant strict obligation to behave accordingly. Kohlberg's observations of collective-norm development support the notion that not *all* actual individuals need cognize the roots of their sense of dignity in order for that dignity to be accepted universally as an ideal of personhood. They also support both my view of the individual as the initial source of social values and ideals, and a concept of prescriptive values as bestowed through social acceptance of those ideals.

The distinction between the rational creation of the ideal of dignity (as constructed upon innate properties) and its rational bestowal as a moral conception that we accept as valuable is key to recognizing a conception of people, rather than an innate fact, as the basis upon which we prescribe rights. Though the conception of people as dignified may underlie prescriptive value, it is not prescriptive value; it is a moral description, or metaphor. Kohlberg's view of collective-norm development supports this trajectory for the process that brings us rights.

DEFENDING AGAINST THE CHARGE OF
UNIVERSALIST ESSENTIALISM

In defending my ontological theory of rights using Kohlberg's psychological theory of justice reasoning, I have brought my argument to a point at which my problem with universalist essentialism is his problem with universalist essentialism. Fortunately, Kohlberg has addressed this problem not only for the universal conception of humans as dignified but also for the assumption of the universal acceptability, and even generation, of what seems a liberal individualist ideal.

Kohlberg defends the "growing theory and research which employs universalistic assumptions."[43] He does so through addressing the flawed assumptions both of cultural relativists, whose doctrine is about "is," or "about the fact that individual and cultural morals are variable,"[44] and ethical relativists, whose doctrine is a doctrine of "ought," which is grounded on the assumption "that there are no rational principles and methods which *could* reconcile observed divergences of moral beliefs."[45] Ethical relativists prescribe on that basis that "everyone *ought* to have their own values."[46] Kohlberg suggests that cultural relativists fail adequately to distinguish between "custom" and "morality" and that in so doing they fail to see that though "moral behaviors or customs seem to vary from culture to culture, underneath these variations in custom there seem to be universal kinds of judging or valuing."[47] He takes the example of sexual mores to demonstrate this distinction, saying that the "culturally variable customs of monogamy and polygamy are both compatible with the culturally universal underlying moral norms of personal dignity, commitment, and trust in sexual relationships."[48] He points to Elliot Turiel's research on custom and morality, which concludes that "moral speakers and their statements may be products of various cultures, but still, in speaking morally, in the sense of *prescriptively* (rather than as cultural documenters), they can speak with a universalizable intent."[49]

Kohlberg next addresses those cultural relativists who attack not specific universalized principles themselves but the very project of developing a theory that offers universalizable principles. Here he addresses the charge that such theories represent Western liberal ideologies to the exclusion of other ideologies. He does this partly by comparing the Western liberal origins of his theory with the Western liberal origins of method and theories in the natural sciences. He assumes the empirical validity of his findings to be as readily acceptable as that of findings in the natural sciences and bases his defence on the fact that the "cultural origins of a theory ... tell us little about its validity."[50] This defence seems problematic given the unique difficulty of establishing and executing appropriate scientific method in the social as opposed to the natural sciences, where environmental influences are much more easily controlled. Kohlberg mitigates this problem, however, by pointing to the confusion of relativists who think his "assertion that certain moral principles and stages develop universally" is the same as an "assertion that [his] ... theory about [such principles and stages] ... is adequate, regardless of its relationship to the Western liberal tradition."[51] He provides strong empirical evidence to suggest that the stages of justice reasoning, with the principles of justice and of dignity around which they develop, are indeed universal in the way he claims them to be. These are phenomena that he has observed or that, as in the case of the sixth-stage conception of humans as inherently dignified, are logically entailed by his observations. While he claims that these observations are universal, he does not claim that they exhaust the moral principles, or even stages of development, that are humanly possible.[52] Kohlberg responds to the charges of the cultural relativist, then, by arguing that empirical facts, with which the cultural relativist is concerned, are consistent with a universalist position.

Kohlberg says that ethical relativism, or the prescriptive relativist view that the fact of cultural difference demonstrates the impossibility of a universalist position, "rests on a logical confusion between matters of fact (there are no standards accepted by all persons) and matters of value (there are no standards which all persons ought to accept)"[53] and commits the naturalistic fallacy. Ethical relativists commit this fallacy in failing to distinguish cultural from ethical relativism. He adds that they also tend to confuse moral impartiality with value-neutrality. Finally, they confuse "a belief in relativism [with a] ... belief in the liberal principle of tolerance or respect for the liberty of conscience of other persons."[54] It is ironic that they make the latter mistake, for in doing so they see their relativism as required by a Western liberal ideal. Kohlberg points out that the principle of tolerance is itself a universalizable moral principle.

In reiterating his universalist claims within the context of this discussion of relativism, Kohlberg clarifies the sense in which various moral norms or issues are (formally) universal and the sense in which they are culturally variable (in content). This form/content distinction is important to my distinction between the universality of the moral-metaphorical conception of human beings as dignified and the cultural variability of the static (manifest-symbolic) and fluctuating (manifest-derivative) norms that emerge from it. For the conception of people as innately dignified is the central universalized tenet of "a universalistically valid form of rational moral thought process which all persons could articulate, assuming social and cultural conditions suitable to cognitive-moral stage development ... the ontogenesis [towards which] ... occurs in all cultures, in the same stepwise, invariant stage sequence."[55] Specific privacy, autonomy, and dignity norms which are constructed from this central norm, however, are culturally variable.

One of the chief objections to Kohlberg's universalism is well articulated by Matthew J. Kanjirathinkal in his *Sociological Critique of Theories of Cognitive Development*.[56] Kanjirathinkal tells us that "cross-cultural studies and comparative anthropological investigations ... do not prove the validity of the developmental assumption itself,"[57] an "assumption" he takes to include certain Western, liberal value judgments regarding such things as simplicity and complexity (i.e., that it is better "to have a complex technology [or culture] ... than to have a simple one").[58] That things develop, however, would seem to be less a radical assumption than an empirical platitude. Individuals, cultures, solar systems: anything that does not die develops. Certain of their developments are generative and certain are degenerative. Because we in Western culture do not like death, we tend to think of generative developments as good and degenerative developments as bad. In cultures where death is not minded so much, it is not generally thought of as strictly degenerative but rather as part of a cycle of generation. Let's apply this to the matter at hand.

Kanjirathinkal's real concern is that it is wrong to assume that what is more developed is somehow better than what is less developed: to do so implies that cultures without the means to progress along Kohlberg's stage scale are somehow morally not as good as, say, Western culture. But this is not implied either by the (later) Kohlberg or by me. The tendency of moral development is to make us more concerned with others since morality by definition involves our relations with others. Moreover, by definition morality sees increased respect for others as positive. To say this, however, is not to say that a morally more developed culture (or individual) is positive in the sense of being better but simply that the culture (or individual) has, to this point, generated greater moral development along a universal scale (perhaps due to material advantages). The less-developed, or "simpler," culture, then, if it is not dying, may also be morally generative (developing). The cultures can be valued equally, because both are generative, even though one has generated more developments. In her defense of Kohlberg, entitled "Cross-Cultural Research on Kohlberg's Stages," Carolyn Pope Edwards reminds us that, in some later work, Kohlberg denounces the notion that his theory can be used to establish the comparative moral worth of cultures.[59] I hope to have shown how this might be so by distinguishing moral worth as being linked to moral generation rather than specifically to moral stage development.

But this will not satisfy Kanjirathinkal, who thinks that "a universalistic position demands a universalistic thinker who can view society from a point outside his/her culture and time."[60] Why so? Can we not conceive historical and personal developmental experience as providing an increasingly univeralistic point of view? The assumption Kanjirathinkal makes here is that universalism and empiricism are mutually exclusive: that we cannot make universalist claims on the basis of empirical data because new data might emerge to subvert our claims. Such an assumption is both epistemologically and scientifically naïve. Of course we can make universalist claims on the basis of experience, ever ready to temper those claims in the face of new subversive data, and ever increasing the probability that those claims are true by finding new supportive data. That is precisely what Kohlberg and his proponents have done, constantly improving their methods, gathering more and more cross-cultural support, to the point where "a good deal of empirical evidence exists to support the cultural universality of 'hard' moral stages 1 to 3 or 4 ... [and this] establishes a strong plausibility of culturally universal moral judgment stages."[61] Kohlberg's critics admit this.[62]

While Kohlberg does not explicitly state the central role of a conception of human dignity within the structure of justice reasoning, he nonetheless evokes it implicitly, through the example he provides of a universal norm having variable prescriptive manifestations. He tells us that whether one subscribes to a moral norm of private property or of public property, "the property norm *per se*, regardless of its culturally variable content-based definitions, is a moral norm found in all cultures."[63] Moreover, and more importantly, he claims to be concerned with "the development of those structures of justice reasoning which can invoke the relevance of the property norm or other norms, regardless of how they are defined substantively."[64] The relevance of the property norm is, of course, born of the universally overarching relevance of justice – interpreted by Kohlberg "as equity or equal respect for all people."[65] One's position on the matter of property, then, reflects one's view of how the dignity of persons is most appropriately served.

Implicit in my defence of the distinction between universal ritual natural rights and culturally relative "trade" natural rights are Kohlberg's conclusions of his defence against relativist charges of universalist essentialism. He claims simply that "the development of structures of justice reasoning is a universal development"[66] and that certain moral norms and elements, including a view of humans as dignified, "are norms and elements that have been used by moral reasoners in all the cultures"[67] he has studied. Given his arguments, in conjunction with arguments I have put forward in support of my theory of natural rights, I find these claims acceptable.

## THE NATURALISTIC FALLACY REVISITED

It remains to distinguish more clearly the difference between Kohlberg's goal in developing a psychological theory of the stages of justice reasoning and my goal in developing a theory of the ontological structure of natural rights. This I shall do by situating my view both within and beyond Kohlberg's theory. First, however, I shall comment on the parallels between and distinctions among our respective defences against the charge of committing the naturalistic fallacy.

I have already shown that Kohlberg regards the naturalistic fallacy as grounding ethical relativism and sees that "as it is practised by psychologists, it is the direct deriving of statements about what human nature, human values, and human desires *ought to be* from psychological statements about what they *are*."[68] Kohlberg accepts the strength of this fallacy and the fundamental distinction between the natural as descriptive and the moral as prescriptive. Here, then, is a fundamental distinction between my view and his; for though I accept the strength of the fallacy as delineated by Kohlberg, I see the moral as initially metaphorically descriptive and hence ontologically subsequent to the innate properties it describes, and as prescriptive on the basis of concrete symbolic representations of these value-laden metaphors.

Kohlberg identifies three types of naturalistic fallacy, two of which he does not commit and one of which he does. He does not, we are told, derive "moral judgments from psychological, cognitive-predictive judgments or pleasure-pain statements,"[69] meaning that he does not base prescriptive morality (or obligation, or legitimate rights) on the valuing of pleasure as "good" or of pain as "bad." He does not assume, then, that moral judgments are "really something else."[70] While one might wish to say that I have assumed this by grounding rights ultimately in our desire that innate privacy and autonomy should be valued, I have not. For on my view moral judgments are prescriptive, being constructed to symbolize manifestly a metaphorical moral description or ideal. Such a metaphorical description is not a judgment but is, rather, a moral principle: "All humans are inherently dignified." I have, of course, argued that moral prescriptions are actually symbolic descriptions of the metaphor of dignity; I refer not to their content, however, but to their form. They are indeed moral prescriptions; they come about through the reconstruction of dignity. Because they are concrete symbols, however, they defer the fallacy charge.

Kohlberg tells us that "moral principles are active reconstructions of experience; the recognition that moral judgment demands a universal form is neither a universal a priori intuition of humanity nor a peculiar invention by a philosopher but, rather, a portion of the universal reconstruction of judgment in the process of development from Stage 5 to Stage 6."[71] In saying this he rejects two separate assumptions commonly made by philosophers attempting, as philosophers must, to construct rather than merely to analyze or clarify a rational morality. The first is the assumption "that a rational system for moral choice must consist of deductions from principles that are self-evident to an actor who accepts nothing but rational methods of inference,"[72] and the second is the assumption "that moral principles are dimly intuited by the common human being ... and the philosopher's task is simply to codify and make consistent the morality derived from these principles."[73] In saying that the six-year-old has a "sense" of his self-importance that reflects both his culture's ideal of dignity and his own innate privacy and autonomy, I may seem to align myself with this latter, Kantian assumption. But I do not assume that my task as a philosopher is to codify the moral world as given in birth through the view of it that I construct; rather, my task is to construct a view that, like Kohlberg's, recognizes that moral principles are not given in birth (hence my "two ontologies"), however necessarily we may arrive at them given the opportunity. In this, then, have I taken up the task of philosophers as Kohlberg conceives it.

The second type of naturalistic fallacy that Kohlberg does not commit is assuming "that morality or moral maturity is part of biological human nature or that the biologically older is the better."[74] This seems to speak for itself given that Kohlberg's theory, and especially that part of his theory that I use to support my theory, is about cognitive rather than biological development and maturity. That certain cognitive advances cannot be made without certain biological advances does not necessitate the inverse, that biological advances entail every possible cognitive achievement at that level.

This brings me to the form of the naturalistic fallacy that Kohlberg admits to committing: "Every constructive effort at rational morality, at saying what morality ought to be, must start with a characterization of what it is, and in that sense commits the naturalistic fallacy."[75] While this is not the naturalistic fallacy as I conceive it, arguing as it does from moral facts to moral prescriptions, it does reflect another parallel with my theory. We both make statements about what morality is in that we both prescribe acceptance of a certain view of the moral world, in the interests of grounding moral judgments. My earlier defence against the charge that I commit the naturalistic fallacy, in terms of the metaphorical and symbolic status of the construction of duties, I have evoked again in defence against what Kohlberg labels the "first" sort of fallacy. Kohlberg's empirical findings about the centrality of human dignity to morality and about dignity's being a cognitive construction rather than a fact of human nature given in birth have lent support to this defence as well as to the role I see for the conception of human dignity within two ontologies of natural rights. Similarly, his claims about the validity of certain moral world-views lend support to the validity of my moral world-view: "The fact that my conception of the moral 'works' empirically is important for its philosophic adequacy."[76] I shall demonstrate the adequacy of my own theory in chapter 5. Here I pose and attempt to resolve the problems of natural rights theories by using elements of the "new moral psychology," which Kohlberg sees as "parallel" to normative ethical theory in the sense that the "psychological description of moral stages corresponds to the 'deep structure' of systems of normative ethics."[77] I suggest that the end-point of Kohlberg's view of cognitive moral development, a point at which rational people universally conceive all individuals as equal in dignity, is the starting point of an ideal that grounds the universal bestowal of original rights.

## KOHLBERG'S USEFULNESS SUMMED AND THE POINT OF DEPARTURE CLARIFIED

I am not a scholar of Kohlberg's theory; but certain aspects of it parallel or support aspects of my own theory of natural rights. Hence his theory is useful in providing both empirical and theoretical support for the notion that one should accept my view of the moral world, particularly insofar as a universal conception of human beings as innately dignified is central to that view, and insofar as the formulation of that conception is seen to instigate a second, moral ontology at work within the structure of natural rights. I shall clarify how Kohlberg's sixth stage of justice reasoning development parallels and supports my conception of moral ontology as instigated through the universal conception of human beings as dignified.

As noted earlier, Kohlberg and I have both had to defend our theories against two charges of committing the naturalistic fallacy. While we both admit to committing it, and justifiably, in producing a standard of moral judgment that is grounded in a depiction of the moral world, we both deny committing it in the sense of arguing that moral judgments are prescriptive judgments logically derived from biological or psycho-emotional facts. Our reasons for denying this are similar, though not identical, because Kohlberg does not attempt to evoke the metaphysical roots of the universal moral nature he describes; this meta-ethical pursuit is one in which I engage, and the nature of the pursuit is responsible for the seeming difference between my view of how we construct a conception of people as innately dignified and Kohlberg's view.

If we review Kohlberg's and my defences against the charge that we see moral judgments as "really something else," in the sense that they are judgments about what causes pleasure and pain in either a physical or an emotional way, we see a reflection of our differing goals. In my defence, though the conception of people as innately dignified metaphorically represents innate privacy and autonomy, it is not a prescriptive judgment about those innate properties (duty not being given in the metaphor); rather, it is a rationally achieved way of conceiving the meaning of those properties for our lives. I argue that the prescriptive norms constructed upon dignity are themselves symbolic descriptions, which "add" prescriptivity to what they describe. Dignity, then, is not something given in birth and named, or "codified," by the few; it is, rather, a construction of meaning accepted universally as a construction that everyone would create given the cognitive-developmental opportunity.

While Kohlberg maintains the same universality and centrality of the conception of human dignity to justice reasoning (morality), he nonetheless views that conception as part of a reconstruction of experience. His goal, then, is to depict the universal construction of moral experience. Kohlberg's is the project of an empirical psychologist. Mine, however, is the meta-ethical project of depicting both how that universally constructed morality reflects perceivable innate aspects of ourselves and how it determines meaning in our lives. Kohlberg sees the principled Stage Six view of dignity as built upon the contractual Stage Five view of mutual respect; I see it as buildable in this way only on the basis of innate properties, and only as a metaphorical description of those properties. Innate properties must be non-moral because morality is a construction: a cognitive construction of experience, a metaphorical construction of the inner self.

Kohlberg himself implicitly acknowledges both the difference in our approaches and the validity of my approach in his postulation of a "soft hypothetical" seventh stage "in the development of ethical and religious orientations … which are larger in scope than the justice orientation which our hard stages address."[78] He states that to answer such questions as "Why be moral?" we must "move beyond the domain of justice and derive replies from the meaning found in metaethical, metaphysical, and religious epistemologies."[79] He speaks of the culmination of such ethical soft-stage development as providing a "nondualistic sense of participation in, and identity with, a cosmic order"[80] and points to the fact that from this cosmic perspective the "postconventional principles of justice and care are perceived within what might be broadly termed a natural law framework ... [in which] moral principles are not seen as arbitrary human inventions ... [but as] principles of justice that are in harmony with broader laws regulating the evolution of human nature and of the cosmic order."[81] It is within such a framework that I work to depict the meaning of human dignity both for human lives and for human conceptions of what our lives mean within cultures, and within the cosmos. I must reiterate, however, that though I see moral principles as non-arbitrary inventions, they are nonetheless human inventions in the sense of being experience-based metaphorical constructions.

# 4 Why Privacy?

In this chapter I shall reinforce the position I argued in chapter 2 on privacy as distinct from, yet interdependent with, autonomy within the structure of natural rights. Thus far I have shown that privacy and autonomy are integrally connected through the moral conception of human beings as dignified. I have defended the universal character of that conception as well as its origins in non-moral properties, its metaphorical status, its role as instigator of "the moral" within the two ontologies of natural rights, its universality (essentialism), its pivotal location within several theories of human morality and moral obligation, and its ability to stand as a gateway from the innate to the bestowed, being itself that which is innately bestowable. I have also demonstrated the interdependence of privacy and autonomy when they emerge from that conception in the form of socially sanctioned ideal rights.

My ultimate purpose, however, is to situate our right to privacy within this structure of natural rights and to show how the structure so conceived can function to determine the legitimacy of specific trade claims to privacy. While he clearly links autonomy with dignity, Kohlberg makes no mention of a distinct and specific role for privacy within that concept. Any attempt to explain why he does not include privacy explicitly within human dignity would be speculative, but it is safe to assume that he holds one of the more traditional views of privacy that it is my goal here to question. Meanwhile, privacy theorists, such as Wasserstrom, who do link privacy with dignity, have generally emphasized the distinctness of privacy by treating autonomy as a separate matter. In my view, autonomy, though distinct from privacy, is not a separate matter when it comes to human dignity and natural rights. This I demonstrated in the second chapter, where I examined the pre- and post-bestowal interdependence of privacy and autonomy. Now I must show what Kohlberg does not, namely, that privacy and autonomy, both necessary to the evolution of rights, are distinct not only at the moral-metaphorical level, within the concept of dignity that is constructed upon them, but also at the post-bestowal level of trade rights, and at the pre-moral level, within the individual.

It is my goal to defend the distinction between privacy as "concealment," and autonomy as "agency" for these two levels. While my theory of the ontological structure of rights contains five, rather than three, distinct levels, I omit both the manifest-symbolic and the subsistence-norm levels because they are very closely linked to the moral-metaphorical, which I discussed in the previous chapter. The reader will remember that the manifest-symbolic level follows immediately upon the moral-metaphorical, and comprises the construction of static norms, or symbolic rights, that concretely represent the moral-metaphorical conception of humans as dignified. The fourth level of the structure, it will be remembered, comprises the construction of concrete subsistence rights, which are related to the body's status as a concrete symbol of dignity upon which to construct prescriptions. All these symbolic norms are so closely related to the metaphor of dignity as to have been addressed through my discussion of privacy distinctly as concealment at the moral-metaphorical level. The pre-moral and post-bestowal levels, however, contain facts and fluctuating norms, respectively, which do not fall under our metaphorical construction of human dignity. Hence they must be addressed separately, as also possessing a distinct element of privacy as concealment.

I shall achieve my end by addressing two charges. First is the notion of privacy distinctly as concealment at the post-bestowal level. While I have already answered the negative-freedom theorists on this matter, it remains to answer reductionist theories such as William L. Prosser's[1] and Judith Jarvis Thomson's.[2] I shall then add new arguments to reveal privacy as a distinct, original right of individuals and therefore as distinct within individuals, as an innate property. These arguments will expose flaws in the theory of Ferdinand Schoeman,[3] who claims that the right to privacy evolves only within specific sorts of communities. Although his historical approach finds the source of this right in Community, it contrasts with the strict communitariarism of Melden,[4] who argues that we are born with rights by virtue of being born into moral community. In the end I will have shown that privacy *is* a distinct and integral part not only of the conception of humans as dignified but also of the natural rights born of that conception and of the natural properties from which that conception is, in turn, born.

### PRIVACY AS CONCEALMENT AT THE POST-BESTOWAL LEVEL

Besides those who see privacy and the rights associated with it as negative freedom, there exists a group of theorists who view any alleged right to privacy as reducible to other sorts of legally and socially sanctioned rights. William Prosser, for instance, has identified four distinct kinds of invasion and three distinct kinds of interest protected through "privacy" claims.[5] For him, what is at stake in a privacy claim is not some vague notion of inviolate personality but our specific interests in reputation, emotional tranquillity, or proprietary gain.[6] Judith Jarvis Thomson views all legitimate privacy claims as reducible to proprietary interests or to other rights, including property in one's person.[7] Neither views privacy as a coherent and distinctive value.

In fairness to Prosser and Thomson, neither claims, in the articles on privacy cited here, to be doing foundational work on rights. It is therefore conceivable that they are simply explaining the relationships between rights and kinds of rights within the trade. Prosser's work, for instance, is a "legal analysis" in which he identifies "not one tort, but … four"[8] as comprising the law of privacy. Clearly such analysis need not explore how our right to privacy comes about.

Thomson, however, does make specific claims about the origin of our right to privacy. She argues both that it is reducible to other legal rights and that it originates in other legal and moral rights.

She tells us that "the right to privacy is derivative in this sense: it is possible to explain in the case of each right in the cluster how we come to have it without ever once mentioning the right to privacy."[9] The rights "in the cluster" are identified by Thomson as those generally claimed under the rubric of our possessing a right to privacy. They include, among others, the right not to be tortured, which we possess because we have a right not to be harmed; the right that one's pornographic picture not be torn, which we possess because we own the picture; and the right to do a somersault now, which we possess because we have a right to liberty. While these examples do not adequately represent rights we might claim on the basis of a right to privacy, Thomson nonetheless says that "it is because I have … [these other] rights that I have a right to privacy.[10] Although she does not claim to be engaged in foundational work on rights, Thomson clearly rejects the possibility that our right to privacy is itself foundational.

Given the limited scope of what Prosser and Thomson purport to do, I shall simply borrow from them the conception of our right to privacy as reducible to other rights. In Thomson's case, I borrow also a notion of our right to privacy as existing only at the trade level, within our other rights. This is what I here reject. Throughout my discussion I shall refer to the "reductionists," meaning anyone who holds such a view.

I suggest that reductionist claims have maintained their strength through the lack of clear analysis on the part of their opponents. Proponents of privacy as grounded in human dignity have not explained just what is at the core in trade claims to privacy or just how "inviolate personality" both subsists, originally, and comes to be, cognitively, within people of all cultures through a psychologically based ontology of morality.[11] While I have already presented these explanations, it remains to apply my analysis in direct response to reductionist claims. Privacy's subsistence as distinct from autonomy within the moral-metaphorical conception of dignity is critical to this discussion. So also is the distinction between innate privacy, as the seed of a right, and the privacy rights that are constructed on the basis of the ideal of dignity that grows from that seed. The matter here, of course, is to distinguish privacy rights not only from autonomy rights but also within other sorts of fluctuating rights. Fundamental, however, to privacy's distinctness within the trade is its distinctness both innately and at the ontological level at which it is first conceived morally.

For given that innate privacy, the privacy of thought production, is inviolable except through the erasure of personal identity, it is not difficult to see how inviolate personality, or the sacred self, might be considered irrelevant to the establishment of rights within the trade. Why, once again, would we protect something inviolable? Yet those theorists who have established a link between privacy rights and human dignity have been correct to suggest that there is something deeper than the trade at the core of privacy claims and that at least part of that core is human dignity. The vagueness of the relation between privacy and dignity thus far established, however, has made it difficult to see how human dignity constitutes the coherence of privacy claims. As a result, it has been possible for some theorists to view privacy claims, taken as a whole, to be reducible to other trade claims.

Such theorists have recognized neither the distinction nor the relation between inviolate personality as it exists originally, through impenetrable privacy and autonomy, and inviolate personality as it is constructed upon that original state in a unifying moral-metaphorical conception of human dignity. They have not recognized that penetrable inviolate personality is a universal manifest-symbolic construction of the human mind that represents to us our reverence for what is innate and inviolable about us. Though inviolable personality is a twofold fact – comprising innate autonomy and innate privacy – there is nonetheless a distinct aspect of inviolable personality for which we show reverence through privacy claims. Such claims we defend morally on the basis of their moral manifestation as metaphor, in human dignity. As I have argued throughout, the conception of human dignity, through the static norms that are constructed upon it, functions to reinforce self-reverence by rendering possible the transgressions that self-reverence demands we forbid.

Through the distinctness of privacy as an aspect both of the inviolable personality of our biological birth and of the metaphorical inviolate personality of our moral birth, we come to a view of the distinctness of the privacy claims that are constructed at the post-bestowal level of bestowed rights. All privacy claims share the coherent aim of protecting, ideologically, the sacred self, a self that we conceive ritually as sacred on the basis of its factual inviolability. At the manifest, trade level, however, though transgression of privacy through transgression of the dignity of concealment is possible, we will never find an example of privacy invaded to the point of the full violation of the sacred self.

No act of transgression, other than ultimate mind control, can ever fully penetrate and expose inviolate personality. Transgressions, however, have both a concrete and a symbolic aspect. As symbols, they come constantly near the sacred core: every forbidden transgression of a manifestation of metaphorical dignity represents symbolic transgression, or a forbidden attempt, against inherent privacy. Moreover, because the dignity of concealment, as it inheres in the moral conception of humans as dignified, generates manifest dignity norms related to the extended self (the body or the private life), it becomes possible to find names other than "privacy" for rights claimed on the basis of those norms. What is privacy originally is bestowed as a form of dignity; that form of dignity finds a multitude of manifest expressions through the social establishment of norms. Dignity so conceived, however, is not too vague or remote a notion to explain our right to privacy; for that right *is* bestowed as a coherent and distinct aspect of dignity.

It may now be possible to understand how reductionists can so convincingly argue for the non-distinctiveness of a right to privacy. In telling us that such a right reduces to reputation, emotional tranquillity, or proprietary interests, these theorists mistakenly view certain trade manifestations of the dignity of concealment as irreducible. They neglect to see that when the layperson claims a right to privacy, as grounds to protect personal information, he never is claiming the right to protection of reputation as it would be seen under the tort of defamation.[12] Regardless of whether this is the law that will provide such protection, the layperson, or all persons, claim the very right to privacy that underlies the protection of reputation and the transgression of which is a reason for the disturbance of emotional tranquillity.

Thomas Scanlon's strong case against Thomson supports this aspect of my view.[13] Scanlon provides an "outline" for a theory of privacy wherein we are thought to possess a "zone of privacy" within which "we can [expect to] carry out our activities without the necessity of being continually alert for possible observers,"[14] and which it is wrong for others to make attempts to transgress.

Interestingly (and helpfully), he claims that social rules "defining such a zone by specifying when and where certain forms of observation are ruled out ... are conventional in [the sense that] ... our zone of privacy could be defined in many different ways,"[15] such as culturally different ways. Scanlon holds that within Western culture, which forms the context for his analysis of Thomson's reductionist claim regarding ownership rights, "ownership, while sometimes relevant to questions of privacy, does not have the importance Thomson claims for it."[16] He demonstrates that it is not the ownership of objects – a pornographic picture, a safe, or, by implication, a house – that makes training an x-ray device on my house and through my safe wrong but rather my possessing a conventional "zone" of privacy. To expand his examples, one might imagine oneself staying in a friend's house while the friend is away and having someone train an x-ray device through the window of the house and through the safe upon which sits the television one is watching. If I am the one sitting in this space, it is at the very least (and more keenly) my privacy that is transgressed and not only my friend's. So, while "ownership is relevant in determining the boundaries of our zone of privacy ... its relevance is determined by norms whose basis lies in our interest in privacy, not in the notion of ownership."[17]

Further to Scanlon's insistence that ownership is sometimes a part of privacy rather than privacy's being reducible to ownership, it will be useful to recognize that Scanlon sees the "current conventions" of Western culture to have established a zone of privacy in which the body of an individual is central. It is not the owner of the house but the person in the room whose privacy we transgress in looking through a window. Moreover, I have every right to use an x-ray device to look through you at a subway map on the wall that you have deliberately blocked but no right to train the device on your pocket or into your lap, even if you have stolen the map.[18] Of course, it is difficult to imagine any culture in which the bodies of individuals are not central to privacy norms, or zones.

Reductionists, then, do not recognize that they speak in superficial trade terms about what has generated the torts and rights that they view as irreducible to privacy. They reduce lay requests for "privacy" to the laws that actually represent, rather than "explain away," the privacy requested. Thomson tells us that a person who looks at our private papers or trains an x-ray device onto the walls of our house violates our proprietary rights over our papers and our persons; it is "because [we] ... have these rights that what he does is wrong."[19] She neglects, however, to ask why our right over our persons includes the right that we should not be looked at under conditions in which we can reasonably expect that we are alone. I suggest that this aspect of our right over our persons is grounded in our natural right to privacy. Certain other aspects of that ownership right, such as our right to do a somersault now, are grounded in other aspects of our dignity, such as our natural right to autonomy.

Thus, I close my discussion of the error of reductionist views of the right to privacy. The distinctness of privacy within the post-bestowal rights trade is clouded both by the multitude of concrete trade representatives of that right and by the difficulty of attributing the occurrence of a right to a notion of human dignity conceived as factually, rather than metaphorically, innate. To understand how rights come about, we must first understand how dignity comes about; to defend rationally the post-bestowal distinctness of our right to privacy, we must recognize its distinctness both as an aspect of our metaphorical ethic of dignity and as a psychological innate property of our minds. Otherwise we will find ourselves trapped in a stalemate with reductionists over the question whether humans are innately dignified *in fact*.

## PRIVACY AS CONCEALMENT AT THE PRE-MORAL LEVEL

I now turn to the defence of "privacy as concealment" at the pre-moral level. While I have already argued privacy's distinctness at this level, I here emphasize the function of that essential distinctness to ground claims. I shall support the individualism inherent in my theory by reinforcing my claim that the moral ontology of dignity is *first* a product of universal individual moral reasoning and subsequently receives cultural sanction. Thus, I also defend my claim that the theory applies universally, across cultures, however thin the value of privacy may be within any given context. However "bestowed" this right may be, it is always originally created.

To these ends I shall demonstrate that Ferdinand Schoeman is misguided in his claim that privacy is valued historically only within certain kinds of communities and largely for the benefit of specific individuals.[20] Schoeman wrongly treats as inconsequential both systemic respect for minimal individual privacy and random claims to privacy by individuals within cultures where privacy is not apparently, or at least not strongly, valued. Such random claims, however, are made on the basis of a universally discoverable conception of human dignity. And systemic respect, for even the smallest personal privacy, pays homage to that dignity. Schoeman fails, then, to distinguish the social requirements of the development of universal moral rationality from a conception of the morality of dignity as emergent from social structure. I will touch on a few of his historical examples to show that indeed privacy is at least a value and, in some instances, a minimal right, within the cultures he examines.

### Schoeman's Position

In the seventh chapter of *Privacy and Social Freedom*, Schoeman tells us that privacy as a social category emerges "only when there is a high degree of social and economic specialization, when this specialization liberates individuals from dependence on any group, and where social welfare ... [depends] as much on individual initiative as on cultural rigidity."[21] To sustain this claim, he intends to demonstrate that "a fundamental presupposition of current moral theory – that human nature is revealed rationally, not historically – is wrong."[22] It is important, therefore, that I engage with his argument because it directly contradicts my own view as well as Kohlberg's finding (not "presupposition") of a morality that is rationally constructed, within individuals, on a universal scale. In particular, I will show the limitations of Schoeman's argument about cultures in which privacy does not seem to be valued; I will show that he ignores the presence, in those cultures, of ritually expressive static privacy norms.

I shall also draw attention to the fact that the absence of an environment in which individuals can rationally acknowledge human dignity does not entail the negation of the fact that that is how a morality of dignity comes about. Social structure conditions the probability, rather than the possibility, of the emergence of privacy or autonomy as a social norm.

Schoeman constructs a "historical narrative" designed to show that "particular conditions are met before one is likely to find social sensitivity to spheres and protection from public scrutiny and regulation."[23] He speaks as though the establishment of social norms for the protection from public scrutiny of aspects of individuals' lives is the only viable indicator that society values human dignity or privacy. He describes what he sees as the evolution of the value of human dignity and privacy through the ages. He first describes early cultures, such as Roman culture, in which much that we now treat as private was public. In referring to such retributive practices as saving "individual pride and honour in the face of a wife's infidelity ... by public reprimand of the woman's misdeeds," Schoeman reminds us that in Roman culture "public censure of private conduct was ubiquitous."[24] Such examples do not do the work Schoeman intends. He means to demonstrate that no aspect of life was considered inherently private in Roman culture; public reprimand, however, is a perfect example of punishment through the elimination of the privacy of a given act.

One might counter by saying that to find privacy essential within a given culture for acts of moral wrongdoing is to find that privacy is a social anti-value. Indeed, that seems to be Schoeman's view of privacy in ancient Roman culture. He tells us that "the private-public dichotomy in ancient times was not associated with respect for the private ... Rather the reverse was the case."[25] It was the public that was valued and respected; anything private was suspect.

Regardless of whether Schoeman is correct historically about the absence of an inherently private realm within Roman political, or post-bestowal, culture, we are misled if we believe that privacy and personal dignity were not important to individuals within that culture, or even if we believe that the value of individual dignity was not recognized, at some level, by that society as a whole. Take Schoeman's example of the adulterous Roman wife, which he uses to demonstrate that marital intimacy and conflict were not inherently private for the Romans. Any shamed man could find a public forum to expose his wife's infidelity, and indeed he was expected to do so in order to protect his honour. While Schoeman is aware that there are people today who will publicize their spouse's marital indiscretion, he points out that in general we now view individual sexual activity as inherently private. It is not only that which we do privately but it is also no one else's business: "an atmosphere of tolerance ... prevails [in] our assessment of other people's lives ... many aspects of [which] ... just aren't our business."[26] His point about Roman culture is that the sexual activity of married females, at least, was everybody's business because that culture valued, at the bestowed level of rights, the sexual fidelity of married women rather than the inherent privacy of sexual activity.

Schoeman should recognize, however, that such fidelity was indeed valued *over*, not instead of, the inherent privacy of sexual activity. The fact that male honour could be retrieved through an exposure of infidelity demonstrates a belief that shame could be transferred from a cuckold to his maker through his shaming of that maker. If extramarital sexual activity were not viewed as inherently private, then there would be no shame in exposure. One may object, of course, that the shame is attendant upon the adulterous aspect of this activity rather than upon the activity itself, evoking once again the conception of the private as suspect. Implicit in any shame through exposure, however, is a conception of the individual as requiring privacy to maintain autonomy, whether that autonomy is put to illicit or respectable ends.

If Aries and Duby are right, in their *History of Private Life*, that Roman society feared what was private and exalted public life,[27] then Schoeman is right to say so, given that he uses their work as his source. It was a culture in which the power of public opinion left little room for the power of individuals.[28] Yet that latter power was felt at every turn, as a force to be reckoned with, beaten down, and exiled. As Kohlberg suggests,[29] that a given culture, for whatever reason, does not embrace either the individual as the primary moral unit or dignity through autonomy (and privacy) as an important moral concept does not disprove a conception of all human beings either as inherently dignified through innate privacy and autonomy or as capable of perceiving that dignity and generalizing it to all other human beings. The only thing the potential existence of such cultures does is lend support to the notion that the dignity of agency and of concealment is not factually original and so requires that those individuals who first construct it possess some social power or sway to encourage that it be bestowed universally, as a right.

That Schoeman thinks he has found in ancient Rome a culture in which privacy and the dignity of the individual were not valued bespeaks his failure to recognize that the individual, in any culture, is the primary moral unit for individuals. Whether this manifests itself in a general cultural norm of selfishness, in recognition of others as individuals, or in individual rebellion against a culture in which power is held by those who will not acknowledge individual dignity, it is a fact of human nature. Moreover, the Roman culture with which Schoeman begins his historical narrative does not in fact stand as a culture in which all that was private was suspect. For indeed there was, within this culture, at least one significant bastion of legitimate privacy that afforded the individual (male, at least) a "sacred self" throughout his public life. I alluded to it above, and Aries and Duby mention it in their book, although Schoeman does not: "The symbol, and weapon, of the father's familial authority and social dignity was the will. The will was a kind of confession in which the social man revealed himself fully and by which he would be judged."[30] Within the will, the public reading of which was a significant event, a man not only outlined the way his estate was to be distributed; he could also "insult, post mortem, anyone he had secretly despised, and praise anyone he had esteemed."[31] The will, then, stood as an icon or symbol, as it were, throughout a man's life, of his inner self, of the privacy and autonomy of his individual mind. The "social dignity" that is represented by the will is not the dignity of conquest but, rather, the private dignity of the individual within a social context that abhors and fears the individual.

Thus, within the very source Schoeman consults to prove his case about the non-interest in privacy in Roman culture, there is evidence for the opposite of his case, at least in minimal terms. That Schoeman overlooks the locus of a concern for privacy in that culture allows us to add to his own claims about the "body of evidence" in support of his case that it is not only "controversial, theoretical, and speculative"[32] but also carefully selected to minimize that controversy. That the will was the locus of individual privacy in Roman culture, and that that privacy was the privacy of thought (being the privacy of opinion) instantiates my claim that where there is any concern for individual privacy (and I think there is in all cultures) the privacy of the mind will be protected. More on this in the last chapter.

Schoeman continues his narrative with a summary of the emergence of the "individual" as a significant political player, telling us that "individuals" come to be only in historical circumstances where people find themselves in conflict with social norms. He provides an interesting account of the emergence of the individual, referring to Norbert Elias's psychological and sociological study in *The Civilizing Process*,[33] Lawrence Stone's historical *Family, Sex and Marriage in England*,[34] David Flaherty's historical work on colonial New England,[35] and Lionel Trilling's work on the novel.[36] He tells us that all his sources demonstrate "little" evidence of historical concern for privacy. He employs Elias to show that people had "little need to restrain themselves in ... their impulses, passions, and emotions"[37] and that there was "little ... distinction between the public and private worlds, between the personal and social worlds, between the internal life and the manifest life."[38] Through Stone he tells us that nuclear families were "not much" closer than extended social groups and that the "majority" of people in sixteenth- and early-seventeenth-century England found it "difficult" to establish close emotional ties to others.[39] Schoeman sums up his use of Stone in saying that there was "little" opportunity for intimacy. From Flaherty he gathers that colonial New England had "little" of the sort of privacy that keeps outsiders on the outside,[40] and that privacy functioned there as a "meaningful moral, legal, and social category" at a very low "level."[41] He uses Trilling to help define emergent individuality.

Each of the studies referred to by Schoeman contains two significant features. First, all four refer to how "little" there was of privacy, or of a concern for privacy, not to there having been none at all. Second, they all refer to cultures that were at best "simple" and at worst "abject" in terms of the material and social conditions of life, and to these conditions as having been responsible for the limited concern with privacy. These two features, taken together, help me to establish the minimal cross-cultural and transhistorical concern for privacy that my theory requires, and to ground the claim, rejected by Kohlberg's critics, for a universal human *development* towards concern for human dignity and personal privacy.

Schoeman rightly aligns a concern for privacy with a concern for the individual. That many cultures have shown *little* such concern *is* evidenced by the historical sources Schoeman cites. I have already shown, however, both that individual privacy *did* have a place in Roman culture, where it was ostensibly frowned upon, and that Schoeman's other historical sources do not see concern with individuals and their privacy to have been utterly non-existent. Yet there is a stronger argument still, from within Schoeman's work, for seeing some concern with the individual as historically universal. For if, as Schoeman says, to be an individual and concerned with individual rights is to be in conflict with cultural norms, and if such conflict occurs necessarily (though arguably not only) within certain more advanced historical settings, thus creating a concern for the individual, then it is the case that individuals (not "cultures") determine a cultural concern with individual rights (being the initial source of conflict). Add to this that Schoeman himself refers to "numerous" cases of claims to privacy and autonomy by individuals living in these early simple cultures, and we find a thread of universal, arguably cultural, concern (at lease in the negative) with the individual. Let's look at what he says.

Throughout his historical narrative Schoeman describes cultures that, in spite of material conditions that made difficult the flourishing of individuals and the development of moral reasoning, nonetheless maintained not only *some* static privacy and autonomy norms but also some individuals who recognized their own dignity and established personal integrity by staking claims. He tells us, in order to write them off as insignificant, of "numerous instances in which people violently protested or in other ways subverted their parents' choice of a marriage partner despite the fact that there was no recognized social norm that could provide a rationale for doing so."[42] Rather than acknowledge the significance of such examples for the claims of individualist morality, Schoeman registers surprise at how infrequent such rebellions were and draws from this infrequency a case for his claim that social structure, rather than rationality, determines human morality. Yet rationality's requirement of certain social conditions to flourish does not hand the work of rationality over to social conditions. Rationally constructed individualist morality has existed, in one form or another, in all cultures (Schoeman and his sources demonstrate this); the fact that technological, political, and material advancement lead inevitably, in Schoeman's as well as Kohlberg's views, to the protection of personal dignity (privacy and autonomy) as a social norm speaks volumes about the inherent value of that form of dignity, even within cultures where the possibility of manifestly protecting it, at the bestowed level, is limited. But let's unpack this last bit.

On page 133 of *Privacy and Social Freedom* Schoeman makes a distinction that allows the presence, in the cultures he discusses, of at least the minimal innate privacy that is the seed of rights, even where the explicit right does not yet exist. He asks what he says is a currently "unanswerable" question (one that it is my purpose to answer) regarding connections between allowing that individual experience includes a sense of dignity and "the evolution" of a sense of privacy as a functioning social category. In thinking about this question he notes the difference between the fact of private experience and our valuing protection for certain aspects of private experience.

There is no question that all human experience, at all times and in all places, is private in the former sense. The seed of the right is everywhere. How we come to *value* privacy is what Schoeman says cannot be fully explained, although he states that it is through our sense of dignity, and that it depends upon material and social advancement.

But if, indeed, it is social advancement that brings about a stronger concern for the individual, for human dignity, and for rights such as the right to privacy, then surely it would be at least awkward to imagine that it is not a part of universal human nature to bring these things about (i.e., construct them). For it is irrational to suppose that the cultures described by Schoeman's sources – with their "abject" material and social conditions, where most adults bore the pathological symptoms of parental deprivation and adult mortality rates were high – were in any way humanly satisfactory, or to suppose that any human being subjected to such a culture would not want to change it. And what Schoeman admits and Kohlberg counts on is that cultures do change. They develop, or they die. If they develop, Schoeman and his historical sources all concede they develop necessarily into materially and socially more advanced cultures in which human dignity and rights, including the right to privacy, are revered. Hence Schoeman's transhistorical study bears out what Kohlberg's cross-cultural psychological study has found, that people who have been allowed to flourish materially and socially will construct their own and others' dignity as well as rights to those things such as personal privacy and autonomy that are connected with that dignity. Implicit in Schoeman's study, then, is strong empirical support for the individualist universalism of my theory. Moreover, if Schoeman's findings regarding the link between material advancement and personal right are accurate, it does not make sense to suppose what Kohlberg's critics suppose, that development towards a concern for individual rights is not a universal tendency in humans. To call such values strictly white male Western intellectual values (as many of Kohlberg's critics have) is to put the cart of Western culture before the horse of universal moral stage development given the right conditions.

As noted in chapter 3, while claims to universality are always susceptible to empirical subversion, they are also reinforceable by empirical means. Here I have uncovered in Schoeman additional historical sources of empirical support for the universality of human moral stage development. Indeed, while Schoeman rejects the notion of any concern for individual privacy in the cultures he discusses (a concern I have demonstrated to be implicit in those cultures, at the minimal level required by my theory) he does so in an attempt to show precisely what Kohlberg argues: that material and social advancement lead to greater concern for individual interests and rights. Moreover, I do not claim that more advanced cultures are morally better; rather, they are materially better, socially and morally more advanced. It is not mine to judge the value of social and moral advancement but only to outline some of the values such advancement leads us to construct. Moreover, it will be remembered, the value is in the generation of moral development itself, not in the level of development achieved.

### BETWEEN INDIVIDUALISM AND COMMUNITARIANISM

While my stipulated goal is to defend my naturalist individualist view of the world of rights and, in particular, of our right to privacy against Schoeman's perspective on the history of privacy as having been a culturally determined interest, I admit to the presence of a communitarian element in my theory of the societal bestowal of originally created rights. This element is neither like the communitarian element in Melden's theory, where moral community and its rights are seen to be an original birthright, nor like the element of cultural determination in Schoeman's theory, where the rights to privacy and autonomy are viewed as emerging only from certain types of community. The communitarian element in my view arises directly from the essentialist individualism inherent in it. In my view, the moral dignity of human beings as an ideology originates in the individual's perception of his or her own nature and in the subsequent construction of a moral metaphor for that nature. I see cultures as universally adopting this metaphor because individuals universally adopt it, on the basis of their self-perceptions. Because I see society's bestowal of this right as ultimately born *of*, rather than with, the cultural moral ideology of a universally accepted view of human beings as dignified, my view is committed to seeing our right to privacy (among other natural rights) as emergent not strictly from individual interests in pursuit of a survivable society but also from community (universal individual) interest in pursuing its own accepted ideals.

The ultimate universality of individual ideals causally necessitates the act of bestowal, by any society whose structure allows moral rationality to flourish, of the rights that are constructed upon those nature-based ideals. My fundamental theory of originally created yet societally bestowed natural rights emerges as bearing a communitarian element that, as a direct by-product of the individualism entrenched in it, situates the theory somewhere between those that see rights as original and those that see them as strictly conventional attributes of specific cultures. Thus, my theory merges not only individualism with communitarianism but also two distinct types of "communitarian" view.

This said, it is important to recognize that my view is not communitarian, even though I admit to a communitarian influence, and in spite of the seemingly narrow fact of innate privacy at the core of our rights. The narrow "fact" of innately private human nature is not the same as what is constructed upon it; rather, it is the reason, as it were, for the construction of a complex network of rights and norms that constitute society's interests. The difference between my view and a communitarian view may rightly be conceived as narrow, but it is extremely dense, constituting as it does the difference between rights that are bestowed and rights that are both bestowed and innate, and all that that difference entails.

## CONCLUSION

My purpose, in this chapter, has been to reinforce both the post-bestowal distinctness of privacy as a right and the pre-moral distinctness of privacy as an interest and a value. In distinguishing privacy from autonomy and other interests at the post-bestowal ontological level, I have engaged the reductionists, whose perspective on privacy is limited to this level only. Within the trade, reductionists see privacy interests as reducible to other sorts of bestowed interests or rights. In neglecting to see the development of privacy and autonomy rights, through the universal construction of a clearly definable notion of human dignity, they neglect to see that privacy – in its innate form and in its form as human dignity – is instrumental in establishing the rights to which they attempt to reduce it. The inherent privacy of thought, for instance, is the seed of our rights over our own persons, a seed that comes to fruition only through the construction of human dignity.

I have also reinforced what I see as the obvious innateness of privacy as concealment (i.e., privacy as concealment at the pre-moral level) by reinforcing the essentialist individualism inherent in my theory. This involved rejecting Ferdinand Schoeman's view of privacy, specifically, as utterly bestowed and bestowed only within certain materially advanced cultures. In rejecting his view I have clarified my distinction between the original seeds of rights and the rights that are bestowed through the rational nurturance of those seeds. I also found, in his argument, a strong empirical defence for the Kohlbergian claims I have employed to defend my theory. Though I have rejected the communitarian aspect of Schoeman's historical view, I have also identified a communitarian element within my own theory that is a function of the particular ontological structure of rights herein espoused, and that falls between Melden's view of moral rights as innate through moral community and Schoeman's view of moral rights, or the right to privacy at least, as a bestowed luxury.

Thus, I have now distinguished privacy as concealment at the pre-moral, moral-metaphorical, and bestowed levels, while also demonstrating the error of two major theoretical positions on privacy. Moreover, I have shown how my unifying theory of the structure of natural rights functions to illuminate the source of error within those theories. Proponents of the negative-freedom view of privacy, for instance, mistake the conjunction of the interdependence of privacy and autonomy with their apparent opposition at the trade level for negative identity. Melden, with many other natural rights theorists, mistakes original creation for original bestowal. Schoeman, on the other hand, mistakes a history of conventional bestowal for a history of conventional creation. Reductionists such as Prosser and Thomson, among others, mistake manifest, trade representations of the bestowed right to privacy for that which is represented by privacy claims. Finally, those who agree with me that privacy claims are rooted in human dignity have not adequately defined the nature and structure of human dignity and thus have wrongly assumed its factual innateness to be an almost mystical aspect of human nature.

Ultimately, any view of natural rights, pro or con, must include a clear explanation of what constitutes human dignity. The theory of human dignity, both as a metaphor for innate privacy and autonomy, and as an ideal upon which to base duties, works to explain the error of earlier theories. It also works to establish a means of determining legitimate fluctuating rights that reflect the source of rights in original human nature. I shall demonstrate this latter capacity presently. Thus ends the explication and defence of my theory of privacy as it subsists in my theory of the ontological structure of natural rights. I shall now turn to the bestowal of privacy rights within the Western rights trade.

# 5 Transgressing Privacy: The Theory Applied to Trade

In this chapter I apply my theory to the Western trade in privacy. Specifically, I engage the matter of determining the legitimacy of claims that human privacy rights are transgressed either by the existence of a national medical data bank or by the admittance of psychological counselling records as defence evidence in sexual assault trials. I then address the broader issue of what the theory indicates regarding the privacy of the citizen *vis-à-vis* the state.

I shall provide a clear basis for determining whether specific infringements constitute genuine infringements of unwaivable rites of privacy, being true attacks upon human dignity and innate privacy,[1] or instead are either socially justifiable infringements of trade rights or infringements of other, possibly economic, aspects of private lives.

## ON TRANSGRESSING PRIVACY

Given the unusual stance I take on privacy, it is important to clarify the possible types of transgression of this right. "Trade transgressions" can be distinguished from "rite transgressions" through the basic distinction between infringements of our broad privacy rights to a private life (protected through conventional fluctuating norms) and our narrow privacy "rights" to inherent privacy and human dignity (natural and metaphorical properties protected both ideologically and manifestly through conventional static norms). A broad range of ends, including everything from the service of justice to economic gain, can motivate trade transgressions. Such transgressions involve true infringement of human dignity and privacy only to the degree that conventionally bestowed rights are being infringed. Rites transgressions violate, or attempt to violate (through symbolic transgression), innate privacy, individual dignity, or the universal conception of human beings as dignified.

The distinction between rites transgressions and trade transgressions may be clearer if I recapitulate certain aspects of my theory, with the aim of exposing a distinction between our sense that privacy is protected and the *fact* of its being protected. Understanding this distinction is important to understanding the legitimacy or non-legitimacy of specific claims.

I have distinguished not only two types of privacy norms – static (manifest-symbolic) norms and fluctuating (private life) norms – but also two types of privacy. First is the narrow conception of privacy as a non-created, innate, absolute human property. This sort of privacy is prior to and evokes the construction of our moral conception of human beings as (metaphorically) innately dignified. On the other side of our moral-metaphorical conception of personhood and the manifest-symbolic prescriptive norms constructed upon it is a broader notion of privacy that protects not only the dignity that is a cultural ideal but also all individuals' conception of themselves as being manifestly afforded that dignity.

While the first sort of privacy cannot actually be transgressed, we provide static symbolic protections that function more to protect the conception of human dignity and to make manifest the obligation that symbolizes that dignity. Such static protections afford rights that are conventional in the sense that they are culturally determined and relative but natural in that they are (locally) absolute and protect a conception of human beings that has been constructed upon innate qualities (including privacy, autonomy, and the capacity to hold values).[2] Hence these rights contain both a natural element and a conventional element, given that they are naturally created but societally bestowed. Any right whose content includes this natural element is a right whose transgression constitutes a "rites transgression." Such a transgression represents a forbidden transgression of, or attempt against (given that full violation is not possible), our narrow conception of privacy.

Broader privacy rights, which we claim when seeking a private life, are established not so much to protect symbolically a conception of dignity that is basic to society as to protect each individual's sense of possessing and being granted the dignity to which society's view of personhood gives him or her a right. If we remember that personal dignity, unlike innate privacy, can be transgressed through the prescriptive norms that symbolize it, then we can understand how a conception of human beings as dignified could potentially take on as many meanings as there are individuals. Society protects the basic conception through static norms. Individuals, however, seeking to have their entire persons, and whatever they deem appropriate extensions of their persons, viewed as sacred, must appeal to society for rights regarding all the specificities of their personal sense of dignity. Though privacy rights involving bodily functions tend to be static (defecation, intercourse, arguably childbirth), there are many rights involving the body and its extensions that are subject to the privacy, liberty, even curiosity rights of others and thus are fluctuating rights. The privacy of an unsavoury romp on the beach provides an example of such a fluctuating right. More detailed examples of these will arise in my discussion of specific cases.

Some fluctuating rights are strictly conventional. By this I mean that they are not natural rights, because they are not constructed upon inherent human dignity. They are constructed on the basis of economic, political, and social interests. Yet they are often defended in terms of our natural right to privacy. This is because individuals mistake the privacy of a private life for the privacy of the sacred self. The mistake is understandable given that certain fluctuating rights are constructed from static norms representing dignity and are natural rights. Distinguishing the two types of fluctuating rights can appear to be a matter of personal preference, but it is not.

For though privacy, like justice, must be seen to be done, it is impossible to bestow legitimately all claims to privacy. While some see privacy as innately "done" and "clinched" through static norms, others mistake the universality of a general conception of human beings as dignified and of the notion of obligation to that dignity for the universality of their own unique conception of what sort of private life preserves dignity. They seek the status of rights for certain privileges, grounding their claims in notions of natural entitlement, because they do not recognize the distinction between the private self and a private life. They do not recognize the ironic fact that there is no inborn "right" included with our necessarily (innate) private selves and no necessity included with our rights to a private life. The rights thus far established to protect private lives are not factually original rights but, rather, created rights; though some are created through a legitimate extension of the duty attached to a universally accepted conception of moral personhood, others are created through a (sometimes legally sanctioned) facile extension of the static norms that manifestly symbolize that duty, that conception, and the underlying innate privacy of persons.

Hence while many cannot see their own fluctuating, strictly conventional rights as viably infringeable, indeed such rights are, in some circumstances. The obligation attached to human dignity cannot be applied haphazardly to claims that do not arise from innate properties, and it is the fluctuating, rather than static, norms that are extended when an individual wins legal sanction for a claim that is not based in dignity. The violation of such a legally won right represents a "trade transgression," and it can be morally viable. Though natural rights are no less created than such fluctuating rights, fluctuating rights are only sometimes created truly on the basis of the human dignity that represents the naturally occurring privacy (and autonomy) of people. Thus are some private-life rights "natural" rights, while others are not.

### Transgression Summed Up

From the above discussion of where our rights to privacy fit into the scheme of natural and conventional rights, we glean some sense of the complexity of pursuing the bestowal of concrete entitlements within society's privacy trade. I should remind the reader that when I speak of the privacy trade, as opposed to rites of privacy, I limit my discussion to the specific (Western) culture in which we live and fight for socially recognized manifestations of natural and universally accepted entitlements. I speak, however, not only of our fight for the legal bestowal of private-life rights, in which the whole person and the accepted extensions of the whole person are seen as sacred, but also of our fight for still-unbestowed private-self rights and for our right that selves should be treated as dignified. For sometimes static privacy

Diagram 5.1
Rights and Transgressions

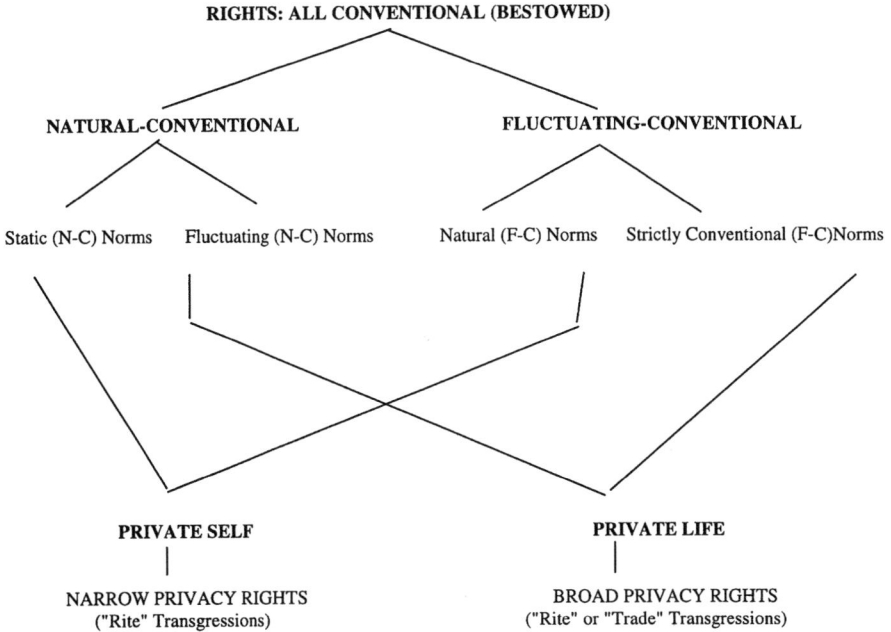

**RIGHTS: ALL CONVENTIONAL (BESTOWED)**

**NATURAL-CONVENTIONAL**                    **FLUCTUATING-CONVENTIONAL**

Static (N-C) Norms    Fluctuating (N-C) Norms    Natural (F-C) Norms    Strictly Conventional (F-C)Norms

**PRIVATE SELF**                              **PRIVATE LIFE**

NARROW PRIVACY RIGHTS                        BROAD PRIVACY RIGHTS
("Rite" Transgressions)                   ("Rite" or "Trade" Transgressions)

norms are not sufficient to maintain the conception of prior human dignity upon which our moral culture is based, so fluctuating
norms must be put into place that remedy that inadequacy. By the
same token, and as noted above, some fluctuating norms are now
in place that do not in fact represent that natural entitlement on
the basis of which they were bestowed but rather reflect other
rights, or alternatively no rights; they are extreme (and successful)
attempts by individuals and small groups to achieve a private life
and become the sacred core of the cultural macrocosm.

   The trick, then, to arguing for the value of specific claims within
one culture's privacy trade is in determining where a fluctuating
conventional (or strictly conventional) right ought to be bestowed
to protect a natural conventional right, and where the bestowal of
a given fluctuating right would be frivolous or harmful to the
social good. While any conventional right (fluctuating or natural)
is indeed a right, it is nonetheless possible to argue for or against
the legitimacy of infringing that right, not on the basis of what
has won legal protection through the privacy trade but rather on
the basis of the degree to which that right actually protects the

sacred self or our moral conception of human beings as dignified. The gauge of viability for fluctuating conventional (trade) rights, then, is the strength of their connection to the conjunction of natural properties and moral ideology, the depth, that is, of their connection to rites of dignity.

Having clarified the types of transgression recognized in my theory of privacy, I shall now engage two specific areas in which privacy issues are currently coming to the forefront of our cultural privacy trade. These are issues of bestowal now being settled by government analysis and policy decisions. The specific decisions being made, however, are, or ought to be, directly related to the degree to which specific claims are grounded in our ideologically deep (or "untradable") rites of privacy and human dignity, rather than in the broader privacy claims of individuals seeking special status within society.

## THE THEORY APPLIED TO TRADE:
## NATIONAL MEDICAL DATA BANKS

I shall first address the potential of a national medical data bank to violate our right to privacy. Clearly, this involves not only the privacy of the body (in some sense) and the confidentiality of the doctor/patient relationship but also broader societal issues of computer privacy and government surveillance. While it is well beyond the scope of this chapter to discuss comprehensively any one of these privacy issues, I do hope to show that, given a benevolent government and adequate safeguards against technological intrusion into the data, a national medical data bank poses no threat to inherent privacy or dignity, in spite of its seeming connection to "the body" and to the dignity of concealment. The purpose for which such information is used bears significantly upon the entitlement of its subject. Even the release of medical information to insurance companies, where patients are aware this is a possibility, does not necessarily constitute transgression of privacy rights.

### The Plan for a Data Bank

David Flaherty, in his article "Privacy, Confidentiality, and the Use of Canadian Health Information for Research and Statistics,"[3] identifies the value of a national medical data bank for assessing the general health needs of citizens and for determining, on the basis of those needs, "more effective services, and better use of resources."[4] He sees "data protection problems" as the chief barrier, from the point of view of privacy advocates, to the implementation of such a data bank. This is a "strategic" barrier: Flaherty's concern is to clear the way for implementation by identifying and recommending resolutions to the problems that emerge not only from the need for actual privacy protection but also from people's need to believe that their privacy is protected. How to meet this latter need is the main focus of the article. I agree that this is the proper focus because I see the issue of a national medical data bank as only minimally a privacy issue.

In his article Flaherty distinguishes administrative from statistical or research uses of information, with the goal of distinguishing true privacy concerns from non-concerns. He advocates the implementation of a "functional separation" between administrative and statistical uses of personal information, citing the *Canadian Privacy Act* to define an "administrative purpose ... [as] the use of [personal] ... information in a decision making process that directly affects that individual."[5] The individual, then, is identified when personal information is collected for an administrative purpose, and decisions are made on the basis of the information. When data are used for research or statistical purposes, however, "no direct action affecting a particular person is ... taken."[6] Flaherty notes that the "almost universal acknowledgement of this fundamental distinction helps to explain the lack of documented concern about statistical matching,"[7] and he implies by this that people are much more concerned to protect their privacy when its non-protection might have some bearing on decisions about their lives. Such decisions might be of a medical, legal, or even economic nature, depending upon the particular "administrator" (doctor, police, or insurance company) to whom information is released.

Flaherty argues, then, that privacy is truly at risk when information is used for an administrative purpose. I suggest, however, that concerns about the decision-making purposes to which personal medical data might be put are not connected to concerns about natural rights. Though many might claim a right to protection against the dissemination of personal medical data to the police, or to an insurance company, or even to the medical community (to use Flaherty's examples), and might claim it under the rubric of privacy rights, they do so wrongly. If we examine each of these dissemination possibilities separately, we will see why this is the case.

Imagine that your doctor wishes to submit personal medical data to a bank for the purpose of making it available to a broader medical community, perhaps including its financial administrators, who can assist in decision making regarding your treatment. You know that you will be identified, but you also know that only the intended recipients of the information will have access to it. Yet you still demand that your privacy is at stake and that you do not wish the information to be disseminated. Just what you view as essential to the protection of your privacy is unclear, in these circumstances. It is also unclear just what constitutes the relation between your privacy and the decisions being made. Under what circumstances, then, might your privacy truly be at stake in this picture, on the basis of those decisions?

Clearly, one's concern about the decisions of financial administrators, acting in their capacity as financial administrators, is not a concern about privacy. For even if one conceives the partial reduction of one's treatment options to a question of economics as an affront to personal dignity, the dignity at stake would be the dignity of agency, not of concealment; the right in question would be one's right to have financial administrators decide, on the basis of one's autonomous right to life, that any and all treatment measures should be taken, not the right that their decision should be taken from them in the interests of privacy. Moreover, though the right to life, as an element of autonomy, is deeply connected to our conception of human dignity, the right to pursue the maintenance of a precarious life, at any cost to society, when the chances of success are slim is not. Such irrational pursuit of life runs counter to our conception of human dignity. The irrationality of attempting to maintain a life that must imminently end runs counter to the rational basis of the construction of rights.

The reader will remember that the ontological structure of rights combines factually innate properties with what comes to be on the basis of human perception of those properties. Our right to life, which is a right of autonomy, is not a right we have against death by natural causes, or even against death by accident. It is a right we have against all other humans that they should not knowingly come between us and life itself. It is a right we construct on the basis of our innate autonomy. To attempt to extend this right in the face of imminent death is to ignore human mortality, which is as innate a human quality as individual autonomy. Such an attempt is clearly irrational, given that not only rights themselves but also their limits are constructed through rational deliberation about innate human properties.

To return to my line of argument, one's objection to the submission of data to medical financial administrators is not an objection grounded in concern about one's privacy but rather is an objection grounded in concern about autonomy. One's fear may be that one's rational pursuit of continued life in the face of non-terminal illness will be thwarted by government budget cuts. While financial administrators should certainly be reminded to take care that readily available life-saving treatment options are not denied to specific individuals, haphazardly chosen, for the sake of cost saving, the desire to withhold personal data on the grounds of this concern seems misguided. Surely no rational individual believes that something to do with who they are could influence their access to available publicly funded medical treatment. Thus, while I have isolated this concern as being loosely connected to natural autonomy rights, to withhold information on this basis is irrational and absurd.

It is also absurd to withhold personal medical information from doctors who are not one's own on grounds of one's natural right to privacy. In their capacity as doctors, making decisions about our treatment, they are the ones we want examining such information. That such a doctor might learn our name in the process of examining our records is meaningless unless we know the doctor in some other context. I address this possibility below. For now I shall isolate just what is at stake when we wish to withhold personal medical data from insurance companies.

Suppose, for the sake of argument, that there is a risk that your insurance company will gain access to personal medical information submitted to a data bank. You plead with your member of Parliament to vote against the implementation of a national medical data bank because you have recently applied for a potentially lucrative (for your family) life insurance policy and are concerned that the availability of your health record might negatively influence the company's decision. You claim your right to privacy as grounds for opposing the data bank. Is privacy really your concern? If not, is your interest purely economic, or is there some other right at stake?

Well, in your insurance agent's capacity as an insurance agent with a decision to make, he or she does not transgress your privacy in acquiring information about your health. Neither is it your privacy that you wish to safeguard against the agent. Your concern is an economic one; you want the decision to be made in your favour and feel that one visit with the company doctor will be less revealing than your entire medical history. The insurance company will argue that it has a right to all medical information it can gather about you, because that information is the basis upon which insurance decisions are made. It is after all a fully accepted practice for insurance companies to send their own medical personnel to examine a potential client. A desire to withhold information from the insurance company for decision-making purposes seems dishonest on your part, and it certainly does not represent a desire to protect inherent privacy or dignity.

Yet it seems that inherent privacy and dignity might be infringed by an insurance company's "hacking in" to a national medical data bank in order to gather decision-influencing information. Do they not transgress our privacy rights in illegally acquiring information about us? Well, no, because for decision-making purposes, we morally waive our right to privacy in these matters when we apply for a policy. What is infringed, when an insurance company "steals" information from a national medical data bank, is the right of those administering the data bank to ownership of the data bank and to control over access to it. It would, of course, be absurd to think that their privacy or dignity are infringed because the information sought is not about them personally. While ownership of the information contained in the data bank remains with the patient, the insurance company's right to that information itself, given that the patient has asked the company to make a decision, is not diminished by the information's being illegally obtained. The right infringed by the insurance company's hacking in, then, is the trade right of control over what one "owns."

In fact, transgression of our inherent dignity and privacy is involved in the acquisition of medical data by an insurance company only when the information is released willingly by the administrators of the data bank without our express or implicit consent. Express consent comprises our agreeing, before personal data enter the bank, to allow the administrators to release such information to our insurance company upon request. Implied consent comprises our being told, before personal data enter the bank, that it may be released to our insurance company upon request. If we have no choice about the data's entering the bank, we at least have a choice about whether to apply for an insurance policy. I shall return presently to the matter of the seeming un-freedom of this choice.

While Flaherty recognizes the importance of consent to the protection of privacy, he wrongly suggests that it is when information is used for decision-making purposes – for example, by medical financial administrators, insurance companies, or the police – that the potential exists to transgress privacy. In the case at hand, however, it is precisely because the administrators of the data bank use the information for non-decision-making purposes that consent is required. The data bank administrators have a right to use the information to make decisions about our health, and the insurance company has a right to use it to make decisions about our insurance; without our consent, however, the administrators of the data bank transgress our metaphorical dignity and attack our innate privacy in using the information they have about us for any purpose but to make a decision about our health. Hence though the insurance company has a right to the information in the bank, it has no right to acquire it; in stealing the information *they* transgress the "data bank's" trade right of ownership (of the data bank), while in releasing the information without our consent, the administrators of the bank transgress our inherent privacy and dignity.

In focusing on the need to protect individuals from the release of personal information to the police, or to an insurance company for decision-making purposes, Flaherty caters to people's desire to extend their "sacred selves" beyond the inherent limits of such selves. The potential for economic and legal repercussions from the release of information is accepted by Flaherty as a viable reason to grant a right of non-release and to call that right a "privacy" right. Yet the potential violation of innate dignity rights is the only viable reason for a privacy right. And how, within a transactional relationship that we freely enter, can our innate dignity be violated when information is used to make decisions about us that we cannot make for ourselves? All three situations here addressed (and suggested by Flaherty) represent "transactional" relationships in which we hand a decision about ourselves over to someone else to make. We see doctors in order to have them assess our physical situation and make the best possible decision (with us, of course) about our care. So although we have a right to privacy, we have reason not to exercise that right if a medical data bank can improve our access to the best possible decision. As long as the data bank is being used to make equitable decisions about our care, or as long as we are aware of any other authorities that may be granted access to our personal data, our dignity is not violated.

By the same token, we stand in a transactional relationship with our insurance company from whom we request that a decision be made regarding coverage. In fact, to apply for an insurance policy is to enter a business relationship that will result in the production of a contract. We do not enter this relationship unfreely. The moral legitimacy of the contract depends upon the client's willingness to disclose fully his or her medical status. While many of us stand aghast at the possibility that our insurance company could, legally or illegally, gain access to medical information from the data bank, it is nonetheless information to which I claim such companies have a right, given the decision-making role in which we have freely placed them. The nature of those violations that are possible under this relationship was established above: only the administrators of the data bank can transgress our dignity, by granting access without informing us. The company can violate only the data bank's ownership rights.

It must be noted that I do not argue that medical data banks are good and that we should therefore accept both them and the fact that our insurance companies might, legitimately or not, gain access to information that, though we do not wish them to have it, they have a right to obtain. For though the companies do have a right to the information, given their relationship to us – a relationship that we have chosen – privacy's needing to be seen to be done may well leave them without a right to obtain the information. Flaherty's recommendation is that the creators of the data bank should indeed promise *not* to give the information to insurance companies for decision-making purposes, thereby removing the only legitimate means of obtainment. Furthermore, current leaps in genetic research that make possible the prediction of countless congenital flaws could eventually put insurance companies out of business, if they rely too heavily on such genetic calculations to turn down clients. We will all die.

The point I wish to make is that the measures Flaherty recommends to ensure that privacy is seen to be done protect interests other than privacy interests, in this case, economic ones. This he must do because people have come to claim protection for economic interests under the rubric of our inherent right to privacy, and because governments are coming more and more to accept the broader trade-determined conception of privacy that is emerging from people's claiming so much under its rubric. This is not, of course, a grand scheme whereby individuals might get more than their due; rather, it reflects a perception among individuals that privacy is at risk in the current technological age, and a (more misguided) perception that the economic self is tied into inviolate personality.

Another issue I should clarify is the distinction that emerges from the tension between the insurance company's right to information about us and the data bank's ownership right to control access to its bank. It will be remembered that on the matter of stolen information, I maintain that the company has the right to the information because our dignity has not been violated, while I also hold that a trade right has been violated – the data bank's ownership right. By this I mean that, while the insurance company should be prosecuted for stealing from an entity that has no inherent dignity to violate, the company still maintains the moral right to use this illegally gathered information for decision-making purposes. This may be an unusual position to take, especially given that in our culture there is strong intuitive support, not to mention legal support, for the notion that people should not benefit from crimes they have committed. But it is important that we identify the true victim of the crime as the data bank's administrative body, rather than the client whose contractual obligation requires disclosure.

Some might object that this position paves the way for anyone to request access to personal medical information "for decision-making purposes." A potential employer, for instance, is someone with whom we hope to enter a contractual relationship. One must remember, however, the unique relevance of such data to the business relationship between an insurance company and its client. Any employer offering a job that requires an employee to meet certain medical requirements for the adequate performance of the job has every right to the relevant medical information. All Canadian teachers and day-care workers, for example, must annually submit a negative tuberculosis test to their employers. The test result is relevant to the protection of people (children) who cannot choose to ensure their health by staying home. I do not advocate that employers be allowed to require medical data irrelevant to the requirements of the job or to the protection of people on the job site whose right to leave is not yet bestowed.

### Personal Medical Data and the Judicial System

I now turn to the third transactional relationship in which we stand to an administrative body. The relationship in which we stand to the police – the third body Flaherty mentions as having a decision-making role with regard to us – is unique in that we do not enter the relationship explicitly, as individuals, but implicitly, as tax-paying members of society. Given our obligation to obey the rules of society, including those generated by our ideology of dignity, we might, under certain circumstances, expect the police to take an interest in our personal medical data. Both the non-explicit nature of the transactional relationship here established, however, and the answerability of the police to our governmental judicial system make it difficult morally to legitimate their access to our personal medical data. The decisions police make on the basis of information either handed them by or stolen from the data bank are not decisions we as individuals have asked them to make. They may, however, be decisions that we as members of a culture holding specific values have implicitly asked them to make. Here, then, we find the real tension between the sacred self and the social good. Note that the source of this tension is the non-voluntary aspect of the relationship of citizen to police, an element also of the relationship of citizen to state.

Is our inherent dignity violated when police obtain access to a national medical data bank to get information in aid of decision making? Well, if we have given individual explicit consent to their having access to that information about us, and if they truly use the information to uphold the laws of the land, dignity is not violated. But what of implied consent? In the case of the insurance company, I hold that as long as we are informed that a relevant insurance company might gain access to the information upon request, the duty to our dignity has been fulfilled. Even if we have no choice about whether personal data will be put into the bank, we do have a choice about whether to apply for a life or medical insurance policy. The transactional relationship between an individual and an insurance company is created by the individual and is contractual.

In the case of police access to the data bank, implied consent cannot be seen to have been given simply through our having been informed; we lack the choice, knowing what is in the data bank, to enter or not enter the specific transactional relationship with the judicial system. We are in that relationship as citizens, not as individuals, and so we might be left in a situation in which government takes information under the auspices of making medical decisions but uses it to make judicial decisions. In such cases we have not, as individuals, chosen that those specific decisions should be made about us. Two matters here have to be decided. First is the matter of whether the individual citizen's assumable commitment to society's ideology of justice, which presumably includes its ideology of dignity, can be taken to override the individual's right that personal medical data should not be made available without explicit or implied consent. The determination of this matter, of course, depends in part upon the second matter to be decided, which is the degree to which personal medical data can themselves be seen to be inherently private. For no ideology of justice that includes a moral conception of human beings as inherently dignified could rationally legitimate the violation by government of that inherent dignity.

The argument I now undertake is designed to show that health information about our bodies is not inherently private through direct relation to "rites of dignity." The argument also goes a long way towards defending the added notion that our thoughts, as expressed in a counselling situation, are indeed inherently private. There are some parallels between these two issues. The acceptability of judicial officials having access to a medical data bank and the acceptability of their having access to personal counselling records are matters of determining how far we can infringe our respect for individual human dignity without also transgressing our cultural commitment to social justice. Both issues require that a clear distinction be made between rite and trade transgressions and that what qualifies as one or the other sort of transgression be clearly understood. It will here come to light that though the information contained within a medical data bank is about the body, it is not of the body and so does not warrant protection through static norms. At best, such data must be protected through fluctuating norms that are bestowed on the basis of current overwhelming pressure upon governments to show that our rights are being protected. I will also show, in contrast, that thoughts divulged to a counsellor do bear direct connection to what warrants absolute protection.

### When the Body Is Not a Symbol

I have taken some trouble to demonstrate how it might be that the body functions as symbol for innate properties we have an inherent tendency to revere. The inseparability of innate privacy and autonomy (and the metaphorical conception of dignity that is constructed to represent them) from their containment in a specific body functions to extend our static rites of dignity to the body as concrete symbol. Indeed, this inseparability makes the body an ideal concrete symbol for more elusive inner qualities that we choose to protect. Hence static norms that express the dignity of the inner self by stipulating the dignity of the visible self are constructed. Though such static norms vary from culture to culture, they all use the body, in some way, manifestly to symbolize human dignity.

Among Western norms are several that pinpoint bodily functions as inherently private; defecation and sexual intercourse norms remain static in spite of fluctuations in public nudity norms. Moreover, regardless of changes in the allowability of certain sorts of nudity, it remains ever the right of individuals to conceal as much of the body as they choose. Our bodies are an inherently private aspect of ourselves and we can express our dignity by exercising our power of concealment. The question at hand is the question whether information about the health of that body belongs to the realm of what is inherently private. It must be remembered that the issue is not doctor/patient confidentiality but the broader issue of social ideology regarding the inherent privacy of such information. I speak of the disclosure of information as a matter of social policy, or of the tension between the sacred self and the social good.

If the body's role as symbol, within ritualized dignity, is to render concrete certain beliefs that we hold about inherent personhood, then it is only through concrete sensory violation of that body, including visual and auditory violation, that we violate the aspect of personhood it represents. Hence while we violate inherent privacy by eavesdropping on people talking to themselves (or to other people), we do not violate inherent privacy in hearing a third-party report of the information gleaned by an eavesdropper. It is the eavesdropper who has transgressed, while I have in no way violated what is inherently private: viz., the "bodies" of the victims as they talked to themselves.

While we certainly maintain both static and legal norms against peering into windows with binoculars, there is no static or legal norm regulating our hearing of a report of what was seen. I emphasize "hearing a report" because a photograph would present another set of problems, given that it provides sensory, visual access to the body, and because no photographs of individual patients are, or should be, contained in medical data banks. Even where the information reported about the body that was seen is used to make a decision affecting the life of the body's owner (the decision, for instance, to divorce a sexually unfaithful spouse), we have no sense that hearing about what was seen in any way constitutes the violation, by the hearer, of the dignity of the body. For violating the dignity of people at the concrete level of the body requires direct access to the body itself; to obtain access to something "of" the body or mind is to take, at the very least, a symbolic step into an inherently private domain. Data "about" us cannot be conceived as transgressing body or mind in this way.

Hence is it conceptually impossible for the police to violate inherent dignity by obtaining access to a medical data bank for decision-making purposes. This is so for two reasons. The first, which I have just presented, is that access to the information contained in such a bank represents direct access neither to the inherent privacy of thought nor to the inherent privacy of the body as the concrete symbol of dignity. Given, therefore, that our social ideology of dignity is not compromised by someone's gaining access to medical information about us, we can turn to the fulfilment of other aspects of our ideology of justice. Here we find the second reason, which is simply that where the fulfilment of our beliefs about justice does not require the (contradictory) transgression of any subcategories of those beliefs (such as our respect for dignity), then we may reasonably proceed to fulfil them.

The first of these reasons may seem to endorse a conception that our dignity is not violated no matter who obtains access to our medical records. And indeed that is, to a large degree, what I endorse (although I will mitigate this claim in what is to come). In emphasizing the legitimacy of access for decision-making purposes, I emphasize a distinction between that which merely does not transgress, but which nevertheless serves no broader purpose in the fulfilment of justice, and that which is truly legitimate, serving, as it does, more global social ideals. While it may seem unfortunate that our medical misfortune (or fortune, as the case may be) may be our legal downfall, it is difficult to see that inherent dignity is in any way at stake when police gain access to medical records about our bodies for legitimate legal purposes. A medical data bank is about the body, but does not provide direct access to it. Moreover, the purposes to which the police will put the information are fully legitimate within the context of our Western ideology of justice.

This conclusion, of course, does not mean that governments might not choose to include rules against police access to a national medical data bank. It means only that in doing so they do not protect inherent privacy and dignity; rather they cater to the demands of an increasingly (perhaps justifiably so) paranoiac public to protect a number of other interests under the rubric of privacy.

## WHEN INFORMATION IS INHERENTLY PRIVATE

I now come to the second current issue to which I have chosen to apply my theory. Although a recent Supreme Court of Canada decision[8] permits, in the interests of a fair trial, limited access to counselling records by defendants, this practice nonetheless violates that which is inherently private. It violates both individual dignity and society's ideal of dignity. What, then, is the difference between medical records *about* the body and counselling records *of* the mind?

The difference between obtaining access to a medical data bank and to personal counselling records is the difference between indirect access to information about an inherently dignified object, and direct access to the inherent privacy of the mind, or of thought. This distinction is the same as that between information about the body and a photograph *of* the body. The information gleaned from perusing an individual's counselling records is of an inherently private nature; to know it is to know the individual's "mind," rather than just something about the mind. While access to initially confidential information regarding one's physical state does not actually provide access to the body itself as an extension of inviolate personality, there is a sense in which confidentially expressed thoughts do provide immediate access to the sacred self, just as there is a sense in which a photograph of the body provides immediate sensory (visual) access to the body.

Counselling situations are "confidential" in a way that allows what is said to bear the status of thought, rather than expression. Counselling sessions therefore fall under the category of things over which individuals have absolute privacy rights. Talking to one's counsellor is not like talking to one's friend because the relationship is designed to promote the healing of the mind through encouraging absolute freedom of the expression of one's thoughts in order that a knowledgeable and objective other might analyze those thoughts.[9] Patients are not expressing themselves to the counsellor but merely thinking out loud. To gain access to the information gleaned by the counsellor listening to this thinking is truly to violate the privacy of thought.

There is an important distinction between a therapist's notes and a tape-recording of a session. A therapist's notes are not necessarily accurate or truthful and so are not deemed to be as useful at trial as a tape-recording. Of notes, however, some might say that they constitute a report about the thoughts of a patient, rather than direct access to those thoughts. They might add that not all that is said by a patient in a counselling situation constitutes the unbridled expression of innermost thoughts. On these grounds they might argue that admitting counselling notes at trial does not transgress privacy, or that admitting at least parts of those notes is acceptable.

A therapist's notes, however, even when they are merely about the patients' thoughts, are intended to assist the therapist in analyzing those thoughts in a way that the patients themselves would do were they not confused or upset or somehow troubled by their thoughts. I suggest, then, that it is the form rather than the content of a counselling situation that constitutes the innermost thoughts of the patient. By this I mean that in entering a counselling relationship, patients can reasonably expect that the therapist's analysis of what they say bears the status of their own innermost thoughts. Some misfortune prevents their analyzing for themselves the disturbance that they feel. Therapists, then, even in writing about their patients' thoughts, function as an extension of the patient's mind for that unique situation.

It might be objected that medical records that are not counselling records also include psychiatric information in some cases. It is unlikely, however, that a data bank will include the specific words of a patient. Focus is more likely to be diagnostic and prescriptive and should in fact remain so. Hence if and when courts gain access to medical records, the information they glean will be about the patient's physical and mental states ("he has diabetes"; "she is clinically depressed") rather than of those states ("she said ...").

There is also the issue of confidentiality where a patient is suspected by the therapist of contemplating murder or other bodily harm to someone. Here the need to prevent violation of our fundamental right to life outweighs our right to privacy for thought. When two rights that are both natural rights conflict, we must determine the respective weight of those rights. Hence while the body-as-symbol (of human dignity) is preceded by inherent privacy and autonomy in the process that brings us natural rights, the destruction of the body is clearly the destruction of those inherent qualities upon which our conception of human dignity is based. To destroy the body is to destroy not only a symbol that represents our self-reverence but also, at the factual level, the biological livelihood of what we come to revere; it is the ultimate symbolic destruction of autonomy, while being also the factual destruction of all individual properties.

But what if records will free the innocent? The decision to endorse an ideology that prefers to conceal the falsity of an alleged victim's accusations rather than to use any means of discovering the truth requires careful defence, especially in light of our cultural tendency to privilege the autonomy of the body; the wrongly convicted will lose that autonomy unjustly. Yet our culture has developed a skewed view of the body as the primary ideological unit of dignity. Analysis of our fundamental beliefs about rights shows clearly that we do still deem transgressing the mind to be the ultimate violation. How ironic, then, that the trade in rights might lead us to imagine that victims should reasonably be expected to submit to being fully raped – in mind as well as body – before they can legitimately seek justice for the crimes against them.

The precedence of the privacy of a potentially dishonest victim's thoughts over the autonomy of a potentially innocent accused's body is a complex issue of "weight" that it is not my purpose to address here. My specific purpose is to show that our right to privacy for counselling records is closely linked to our dignity. That it is more closely linked than bodily autonomy is dictated by our culture's beliefs about rights as they are reflected in my explication of the ontological structure of natural rights. The privacy and autonomy of the mind are the natural seeds of our rights to privacy and autonomy; while wrongly convicted defendants are egregiously violated, and while that violation will certainly bear psychological consequences, they go to prison with the ultimate privacy and autonomy of their minds intact. Victims face the violation of mind as well as body in being forced to submit counselling records at trial. Even if they are lying, other means of uncovering that lie, which certainly do exist, must be sought.

This said, I must mitigate my argument by adding that if a patient tells a therapist explicitly that he or she was not assaulted and is lying at trial, and if it is the therapist's professional opinion that this is true, then the therapist has an obligation to report (verbally) this finding. In doing so, the therapist, in his or her status as an extension of the patient's mind, "confesses" for that patient. Sifting through notes for signs of untruth, however, is unacceptable.

### Summing Up the Cases

If we remember that privacy needs to be seen to be done and the problem this requirement creates in a culture where people tend to get the fluctuating privacy of their lives confused with the static privacy of their innermost selves, of each person's attempting to become the sacred self of the macrocosm, we can see that governments and courts have wrongly accepted this broad bestowed privacy as the true seat of human dignity. Having done so, they are forced to cater to individual conceptions of a private life to a point that sometimes provides undue economic protections and is sometimes to the detriment of the social good.

In such instances, my conception of privacy as an original, or naturally created, right leaps to the aid of the social good instead of providing the hindrance that natural rights, given our contemporary conception of them as imposing absolute obligation, tend to provide. For while I do see control as an integral aspect of having privacy, it seems that if the lonely man on the desert island controls access to at least some basic symbolic manifestation of his inherently private nature – be it a makeshift shelter for defecation or a veil for eating – then his individual dignity, and any intruder's conception of that dignity, will remain intact.[10] He does not need control over people's seeing the island itself or over all the natural resources of the island; the current liberal democratic enthusiasm about privacy has allowed the protection of many unrelated interests under the rubric of protecting privacy. On the matter of a national medical data bank, this error has led governments, through privacy commissions, to be overly generous in the protection of people's subjective sense of their privacy.

On the other hand, releasing (alleged) victims' psychiatric and other types of counselling records to defendants in the interests of a fair trial *does* violate individual dignity and attempts to violate innate privacy. For although this issue is like the data bank issue in that it is concerned with individual control over personal information, "information" in this case is not about but *of* an aspect of personhood that is associated with inherent dignity. This is the case, of course, where the information has been truthfully supplied. To know the body, forcibly, in as direct a way as this is forcibly to know the mind, constitutes what our culture considers egregious transgression of personal dignity. That the body serves to make manifest our reverence for the innate privacy (and autonomy) of thought can sometimes lead us to forget the elusive properties represented in that symbol, and that they are so represented at all. Hence are we faced with the irony of a government's taking extreme measures to protect the illusory "privacy" of medical information that it might be seen to be done, while nonetheless allowing the violation of dignity through the attempted violation of what dignity represents, the innate privacy of thought, which is the foundation of our reverence for the body. This they do so that "justice" might be seen to be done.

The original innate privacy of individuals, which is symbolized and protected through a moral conception of human beings as dignified, though it cannot be fully violated, must never be attacked. Our narrow rites of privacy must never be transgressed. When they are transgressed, the very conception of justice that we hope to preserve, and that is built upon our conception of human dignity, is compromised. For this reason a fluctuating right to absolute confidentiality in counselling situations should be bestowed in order to protect our natural-conventional right to the protection of dignity. Of course, we also have an absolute right not to be wrongly convicted and jailed; I state only that counselling records containing explicit patient statements are not a morally viable source of evidence.

## THE THEORY AS A GAUGE

Brief as my analysis of these two cases has been, I hope that it has begun to demonstrate how the theory herein, of natural rights and of our right to privacy, serves to provide a gauge of entitlement. This it does by clarifying the nature of human dignity as being neither an inherent fact of birth, and thus a blanket license to make claims, nor a political fabrication, and thus the foundation of nothing. Human dignity conceived as a psychologically necessary construction designed both to explain what we innately are and to express our ultimate self-reverence is human dignity conceived as both a potential and an inevitable political construction, which requires that every claim made on its basis be evaluated against every ontological level of the structure of rights to see whether it is truly of that structure.

Through evaluating claims against the structure, we come to a clear view of the presence of the inherent privacy of thought, the most fundamental level of what we revere, in a counselling situation where the type of self-expression required is non-selective, or what some would refer to as "stream-of consciousness." We come also to a view of a national medical data bank as coming nowhere near transgressing, or attacking, those inherent human qualities the reverence of which we seek to express both through static rights of dignity and through the fluctuating dignity rights that are the necessary trade expression of a cultural ideology of dignity. We come to this view through my resolution of another important point of theoretical confusion.

The view of a national medical data bank as not approaching inherent privacy is grounded in the recognition that the body is neither itself factually innately dignified nor, a related point, that from which our metaphor of human dignity arises. This, I think, has been a point of massive confusion in Western culture where the body, which (as an aspect of dignity) is merely a concrete symbol of what we revere, has, through its concreteness and as the object around which static norms are constructed, come wrongly to be viewed as the seat of inherent dignity itself. Yet it is only in its concreteness that the body represents our dignity and the innate properties of human thinking, and so facts about our bodies are not inherently private, even where economic and other social interests might cause us to wish that they were.

### Social Self-Protection: Mitigating the Hard Claims

One might ask at this point whether the embarrassment we feel at the thought of everyone's (or anyone's) knowing certain facts about our bodies does not speak rather emphatically to the notion of the privacy of such facts. But it is not embarrassment we feel when we think of doctors or health administrators or insurance companies or even necessarily the police looking at our health record. For in all such instances I have shown that interests other than privacy are at the basis of our discomfort. On the other hand, were the police to charge us with something and present facts about our bodies in the public forum of a courtroom, we may face the discomfort of knowing not only that there is some biological evidence against us but also that family, friends, and co-workers or employers will now know some hitherto secret fact about our bodies. Perhaps, for instance, we have failed to pay a surgeon for liposuction, claiming never to have had such surgery, and face the possibility that co-workers will soon know the extent of our vanity and of our avoidance of exercise (not to mention the avoidance of paying our surgeon).

Since this is a tricky example, let us first imagine simply that one person who comes across the liposuction fact in processing our medical data is someone who knows us in another context, at church, perhaps, or through a service club. Can this one person's knowledge of a biological fact to which a face, a personality, and a reputation can be attached constitute the transgression of dignity? Even if this person tells no one else, is there the potential for transgression?

The answer to this question lies in distinguishing the uses to which one individual can put such information. If the person in question simply "knows" the fact and puts it to its intended use of improving health care, then clearly no violation of dignity has occurred. Some violation has occurred, however, if this person puts the information to the insidious "use" of feeling the power of knowing about someone something intimate that that person may not be aware anybody else knows and definitely does not want anybody to know. Where patients do feel possessive of the knowledge of their surgery, then, even though they are misguided to think that their dignity is situated in the privacy of that medical fact, their transgressors takes advantage of Western confusion about the body (a confusion in which such transgressors clearly share, and to a greater degree than most) in order to violate the inherent privacy of the patient's thoughts. For in feeling the voyeuristic power that they feel, transgressors are not violating their victims' bodies but rather attempting to enter their minds, assuming that the victims think the information that has been discovered is private. Ironically, were the victims to recognize that their dignity is not situated in facts about their bodies, the silly voyeurs would be alone in their lunacy, unable to puncture any dignity but their own.

If we return to the possibility of our co-workers having access to facts about our bodies, we see that the preservation of dignity is contingent. If our co-workers sought the information deliberately in order to violate our dignity, then certainly a symbolic transgression has occurred. If we are able to feel what we rationally know (and what many cultural clichés will tell us), that our dignity is not situated in those facts, then while our co-workers have committed a moral wrong, we have not been wronged. They have committed a victimless, morally wrong act. If, however (as is more likely), we are too strongly conditioned to forego our feelings of shame at having these facts known, then we are the victim of their act.

If our co-workers accidentally come to know personal facts about our bodies, then no symbolic transgression occurs initially.

Undoubtedly, most will respect the personal nature of the information and think no more of it. A few who enjoy the information may be in the position of the voyeur, who transgresses symbolically through enjoyment of the power of knowing. It is here again the victims who determines their own victimization, although it is not through rational choice that they determine it. They must be able to feel the insignificance of the facts to escape being victimized. Anyone, such as an employer, who puts the information to use for decision-making purposes regarding the fact or nature of employment transgresses an economic, rather than a dignity, right.

While my theory works to clarify confusion and to separate true from false transgression, it cannot eradicate confusion. It can neither eliminate voyeurism nor cause people to feel what they rationally know. But it does offer an understanding of who we are morally, and of how we come to know ourselves, an understanding that could pave the way to eradicating the need for extreme visible measures of privacy protection, and to diminishing the power of voyeurism in the context of a culture of individuals who recognize the body as a concrete moral symbol, rather than as both the seat and the symbol of all that is moral and immoral.

Though medical information is not of an inherently private nature, the individual cannot, at this time, be expected to forego all claims to a right that personal data not be made accessible without consent. For though true privacy is not violated by the obtaining of such data, people's confusion about what is private is not yet clearly enough understood. I advocate implementing the requirement of consent in its weak sense, as implied through people's awareness of the possibility that their files will be scrutinized. I also advocate, contrary to Flaherty's recommendation, that such files should be made accessible to other administrative bodies only for decision-making purposes. Moreover, I espouse Flaherty's suggestion that computer protections must be implemented and enforced in order to prevent, as far as possible, the obtaining of information by people who know the patient and who could potentially take a voyeuristic attitude towards the possession of personal facts about the patient. For however inaccurate our perceptions of our own dignity may be, my theory attests to the power of self-perception to create (at least an individual) reality.

Counselling records, however, are inherently private. They constitute a portion of the innermost thoughts of a counselling patient. As such, they represent something over which a patient has absolute privacy rights.

### Citizen and State

The uneasy question arises just how far the state may go, according to my theory, in gaining access to what individuals deem private. I have eliminated the inherent privacy of medical and, presumably, other types of information for certain social purposes. Yet I also advocate our making "static," for most circumstances, certain privacy rights that are currently fluctuating rights, at the mercy of the courts. What privacy rights have we, then, against the state?

While it would be futile to attempt to catalogue our rights here, it may be helpful to follow the stage progression of the construction of rights to see just what rights against the state are established (or set to be established) at each level. At the pre-moral level, where the natural properties of the innate privacy and autonomy of the mind merely subsist as the seeds of rights, we naturally find what is at core. We find a biological fact – that our brains function privately and autonomously – which, when translated (constructed) into the language of rights, provides the ultimate ground of all rights claims. By this I do mean that all human rights are biologically grounded in the privacy and autonomy of brain function and that they are all, ultimately, privacy or autonomy claims.

This said, it is important to recognize that this biological fact does not give us *carte blanche* to determine our own entitlement. This fact is the foundation of a structure that must weigh and accommodate conflicting claims. Nonetheless, as was stated in the first chapter, this level assures us the privacy and freedom of thought; we must at least have an absolute right to the natural function of our minds. This function is, by nature, private and autonomous, and so we have an absolute right against the state (and everyone else, for that matter) to the privacy and autonomy of our thoughts. Note also that this right is not only a "mental" right, it is also physical, given that the privacy of thought is directly linked to the privacy of biological brain function. We also have a right, then, to assurance that our brains shall not be physically invaded to promote the social good (how this could do so I'll leave to another imagination).

It might be objected that I have claimed biological rights (over our bodies) to be symbolic in nature, coming to be much later in the structure and "merely" symbolizing the privacy and autonomy of thought. I put to you that symbolic rights and obligations to do with the body, while originating with the privacy and autonomy of the mind, are not as directly linked to the mind as is our right to assurance that the privacy and autonomy of brain function shall not be transgressed. Where we tamper with brain function we transgress the absolute right to privacy and autonomy for thinking. We do not do so when we either copulate in the town square or train hidden cameras up women's skirts (a phenomenon I only recently learned about), both of which acts we have absolute symbolic norms against. At the pre-moral level, however, we can establish a basis for only the most fundamental rights against the state, that the privacy and autonomy of our brains/minds will not be transgressed. Included in this right is a right not to be killed, given that biological death certainly eliminates the privacy and autonomy of thought. This is a right we hold against all persons and government as well, and it translates into a right not to be subjected to any concrete form of brainwashing, or to capital punishment.

We come now to the next two levels of the structure of rights at which metaphorical human dignity is established as a value and concrete (manifest-symbolic) norms are constructed to represent that value and our obligation to it. Beyond a general right that our individual dignity should be revered, the specific rights we hold against government at these two levels combined are in fact countless. I will therefore focus on a right around which there may be some discrepancy on the basis of what I have said thus far, and that itself is one of the key manifest-symbolic norms of Western culture. I refer to our right to privacy for defecation/urination.

The seeming discrepancy here is that between my claim that police access to medical records (information about my biological and psychological state) is morally permissible and my claim that we have a locally absolute right to privacy for certain biological functions, functions the police have been known to monitor when investigating drug crimes. Yet the difference should be plain: once again, the medical records are "about" me, and the use to which they are put determines transgression. Like the words out of my mouth to a therapist, the right to privacy for defecation is the right against direct access to something that Western culture has constructed as inherently private: sensory access to our bodies, as to our thoughts, is something we have a strict moral right to control.

But that's not so, some might say. The fact that police often override this "right" in gathering evidence for drug busts "proves" that this is an overridable right. Police install cameras in washrooms, or they wait for suspects to defecate so they can examine their feces for a swallowed stash. Yet this is where we come to the usefulness of the theory in helping us re-evaluate the law; for I refer to the moral right to privacy that is implicit in the Canadian Charter of Rights and Freedoms, rather than to legally entrenched rights. That the police do this, and legally, does not mean they have a moral right to do it. Helpfully, a Kitchener court recently threw out drug charges against a suspect whose absolute (Charter) right to privacy in a washroom stall had been "overridden" by police in the gathering of evidence.[11] There is a tension, therefore, between our ideology (as represented by the Charter) and our common practice on this front. The moral theory herein explicated sides with the judge whose interpretation of the Charter includes an absolute right to privacy in a washroom stall. I agree with this judge on the basis of the about/of distinction outlined here, and other rights can be evaluated in the same way.

Those who claim that this right can be legitimately overridden in our culture (legally perhaps but not, I argue, morally) might also wish to claim that it is a right I may waive, opting to leave open the washroom door. Answering this charge fully would require a fuller discussion of the public/private distinction than it is my intention to engage in; but just try pissing into the fountain at a local mall, or even (gentlemen) leaving open a public washroom door while using a urinal, and the difference will become eminently clear (and don't fool yourself that the only problem in the fountain example is public health). In the public social context of which I speak, "waiving" is out of the question. Just what counts as "public" or "private" is, as I have said, beyond my scope, yet there are (private) circumstances in which we know we can waive, and (public) circumstances in which we know we cannot. The locus of local-absoluteness is that public forum.

So, while reverence to human dignity will have many manifestations in specific rights, this discussion of our right to privacy in a washroom stall provides, I hope, some guidance as to how the theory can be employed to evaluate legal rights, and as to just what sorts of things are protected against government intrusion at the moral-metaphorical and the manifest-symbolic levels.

The fourth level of the structure of rights is the level at which subsistence rights are constructed for all individuals against all others. When I initiated discussion of these rights in chapter 1, I placed them in the context of pursuing international justice for the starving of other nations. I said there that all have a natural right to be fed when they cannot feed themselves. This claim has local implications for the rights of the citizen, against the state, to be provided welfare benefits. If we owe a duty to the starving of other nations, then certainly we owe a duty to those impoverished within our borders. The burden of "proof of need" will, of course, require the impoverished to forego certain entrenched privacies; yet such proof should not require more than access to financial/employment records, records about the financial status of individuals. The government has no right to monitor people in their homes or to go through their closets (in search of a spousal presence, for instance, in the homes of those on "mother's allowance").

Why not, one might ask? The home is surely neither of nor about the body or mind of an individual. Surely this theory renders our homes no longer inherently private because they are not "of" the body or mind. It must be remembered, however, that things of the body or mind are only the most basic things to be protected, at the earliest stage of the construction of rights. At the symbolic level, the home becomes an inherently private extension of an innately private self. Social workers may not simply tour them in search of evidence. Police, however, with a proper evidence-based search warrant, may do so even though they have no right to search bodies in this way. The difference lies in the difference between the body as the factual/original seat of self and the home as a symbolic extension of that self. Symbolic norms (such as our defecation norms) that are directly attached to the body or mind cannot be overridden with moral justification. There can be justification, however, for overriding a symbolic norm regarding a symbol (the home) for the self; someone else's more basic personal privacy or autonomy may be at stake, and that takes precedence over the symbol. This is not to say that our right to privacy in our homes is not as "real" as our right to privacy for biological functions but only that the latter is more deeply embedded in the source of rights.

The fifth and final level of the construction of rights is, of course, the trade level. It includes many legally entrenched yet fluctuating norms that are not natural entitlements (such as the right to keep insurance companies away from our medical records), but it also includes many genuine moral rights, some of which are placed at risk by their proximity to those fluctuating norms. While it is once again impossible to outline all the rights we hold against the state, it may be possible to illuminate a few of the rights we have and, in particular, how to determine that we have them.

Let's return to the example of weighing a victim's right to privacy of thought against a suspect's right to make full defence. The latter right is ultimately an autonomy right since it relates to the suspect's right not to be confined for something he or she did not do. The tension between these rights makes them appear to be "fluctuating," or overridable on the basis of others' rights, when in fact they are both static: one is based in the right to private thought and the other in the right to autonomous movement. Yet if we analyze them still more closely, we see that the right to private thoughts is more fundamental than the right to autonomous movement because the latter is a symbolic right regarding the body as symbol, while the former is a symbolic right regarding the mind itself.

When someone is jailed (and we do have a moral right to jail wrongdoers, although not to kill them) the body of that person is not itself transgressed, only its range of movement. Thus, the body functions in its capacity as symbol, and the state keeps away (or should) from direct transgression of the body. But when the state examines or allows the examination of private thoughts as spoken in a counselling session, it allows a mind to be violated directly. This does not mean that our right not to be jailed when innocent is not a very real, strong, and indeed fundamental moral autonomy right; it is. All I say is that, for those who insist upon weighing these rights against each other (something I have said is unnecessary given that it is morally wrong to violate the mind, making the counselling records rule absolute, and given that such violation is not necessary to achieve a fair trial), the right to a given range of bodily movement is not as fundamental as the right to private thoughts.

The preceding constitutes a very hard and controversial case; yet I employ it to clarify the method for evaluating the moral status of trade norms. The potential for violation must be traced back through the structure of rights to its origin. Some norms will originate at the manifest-symbolic level, making them strong symbolic rights. Others may be traceable to the very origin of rights, protecting the fundamental privacy and autonomy of brain and mind function. Still more will be found that, although they are claimed under the rubric of protecting privacy or autonomy, have little or nothing to do with fundamental symbolic or biological rights. Many of these will be found to protect economic interests.

Against the state, then, we have many individual rights including the right to welfare in times of need, the right to freedom when innocent, the right to privacy for thought and for biological functioning, and the right not to be killed, no matter what. Many more moral rights can be determined to be legitimate (or not) on the basis of their connection to the various levels of the construction of rights.

# Conclusion

It has been my purpose to identify the source of our right to privacy and determine its power to supersede other individual and social interests. To do this I have taken a cross-disciplinary approach to establishing a theory of a universal ideology of entitlement that is best expressed through an explication of the dual ontological structure of natural rights. Inherent in this explication has been an examination of "the moral" as a metaphorical representation of innate facts, which representation serves both to satisfy our desire that our lives should have positive meaning and to ground certain claims that will facilitate or enhance that meaning. Conceiving of moral personhood as a rational, metaphorical construction founded on innate facts has led to a view of natural rights as being both innate and conventional, or original and bestowed. For while they are originally (or non- ) created as non-normative innate human properties, they are societally bestowed as rights.

While my initial goal was to reveal the power of our right to privacy by establishing the ontological power of human dignity, the recognition of this dignity (as a metaphorical construction designed to represent the value of what is innate) has given tremendous complexity to its ontological status; for the power of our right to privacy becomes dependent upon the ontological status we afford to a metaphorical construction of innateness. But how real and therefore how powerful in terms of grounding moral prescriptions is a mere metaphor? The answer is that the metaphor of human dignity, which grounds morality by instigating a moral point of view, is extremely powerful, and universally so, when it comes to the grounding of natural rights. Rights truly based in this conception of human beings are rights that no individual culture with adequate opportunity for individual rational development could reject. For the metaphor of people as innately dignified stands as a universally constructed and accepted conception of moral personhood.

In privacy's ontological status as a psychological pre-moral human property that, with autonomy, grounds the moral-metaphorical conception of human beings as innately dignified, it is very well situated to be something upon which we have a strong basis to stake claims. Important to understanding the limits of our right to privacy, however, is an understanding of the distinction between our static privacy rights, which are part of the ritual construction of dignity rights, and our fluctuating privacy rights, which may or may not be grounded in rites of privacy, and which extend beyond the protection of the sacred self to the protection of a private life. Inherent in any "stepping out" from the self in the pursuit of rights is the risk that we will pursue too much under the rubric of self-protection and will seek rights that protect not an individual's sacred core but rather a conception of one individual as the sacred core of society. This is clearly unacceptable.

Yet I have been able merely to provide direction, through the case studies and through my discussion of the rights of the citizen against the state, as to how my understanding of the right to privacy and of natural rights in general can lead to the resolution of trade disputes. By analyzing each claim against the ontology of rights, to determine its relevance to innate properties and to the construction and expression of dignity, we can find answers. This is because the theory clearly defines both the place of human dignity in constructing rights and the content of human dignity. Moreover, the theory clarifies the role of the body as a concrete symbol, rather than as an innately dignified object, within the structure of moral entitlement, thus unravelling some of the Western world's confusion about its inherent value. The body here emerges as being inherently valuable, at the moral level, in providing a concrete opportunity for protection and, at the factual level, in providing the livelihood of the inner self that we value morally. This has been seen to have implications for claims regarding facts about the body. An examination of the broader implications of the theory for other issues in privacy, autonomy, and natural rights remains to be done. My goal in this book has been to explicate and defend the theory itself in detail, while merely pointing to its practical value.

A matter I hope to expand on at a later opportunity is my claim that the theory represents an example of the kind of philosophical pursuit Lawrence Kohlberg characterizes as indicative of a "high, soft seventh-stage" in justice reasoning development, a stage in which the nature of morality and the meaning of human existence are explored. Indeed, I should like to examine further the implications of Kohlberg's psychological theory of moral development for a conception of human dignity, in order to determine the true depth of the connection, or disparity, between our views.

Certain other matters that are not addressed in detail here might be seen as crucial to a comprehensive theory of natural rights or of any specific right. I have in mind especially the matter of the waivability of rights. Suffice it to say that most static privacy norms, such as the defecation and sexual intercourse norms of the West, are not waivable in a social context. They are, as I have argued, locally absolute. Most fluctuating norms, however, are waivable. Yet there is a category of "grey-area" norms for which it is difficult to say whether they are waivable because it is difficult to say whether they are static or fluctuating. In general, if there is doubt about the status of a norm, it is probably a fluctuating norm and probably has to do with the body. The recent Ontario Court of Appeal decision that Canadian women living in the province of Ontario have the right to bare their breasts in public provides an example of a seemingly static privacy "norm" that turns out to be actually a fluctuating norm.[1] The norm against the waivability of privacy for breasts was established on the basis of a conception of the *female* body as a symbol of sexuality, rather than on the basis of a conception of all bodies as symbols of dignity. The fact that the non-waivability of this privacy right did not extend to males is proof that the dignity of the human body was not at issue and that this right was not, therefore, a static norm. I suggest that such seemingly static but actually fluctuating norms are established through Western confusion about the significance of the body to human dignity and about the status of the body as a concrete symbol of what we revere, which, in providing the opportunity for transgression, has wrongly come to be seen as the origin of indignity. Of course, the wisdom of baring one's breasts, and even the motivation for doing so, within the context of Western culture's current breast-fetishism is both questionable and another matter.

On the other hand, while our right to privacy in childbirth is clearly a waivable right given that medical personnel and family members or friends are often invited to the event, and given that no woman who goes into labour and gives birth in a public place will be arrested for doing so, there is nonetheless some question as to where Western culture would stand on the matter of a planned public demonstration of live childbirth. Because childbirth involves at least a third person, who is also a child, and because we have no control over its happening, it is difficult for us to see it as a sexual act in the same way that intercourse is a sexual act. I suggest, however, that if it became popular to plan public birthings, our obscenity laws would soon put a stop to it; this is because the privacy of genitalia is one of the principal static dignity norms of Western culture, and because an element of control is introduced through the premeditation of the act's being performed publicly.

This brief digression into the relation of the waivability of privacy norms to their status as static or fluctuating does not complete what might be said about the matter of waivability in the theory at hand. But it does provide another way to gauge the status of a right; for just as a right's being static tells us that it is unwaivable, so does a right's being waived, at the societal level, tell us that it is not static.

Beyond the explication and defence of a theory of natural rights and of our right to privacy, I have been able to explain earlier theoretical discrepancies regarding the nature and status of our right to privacy. I have demonstrated how some of the key earlier theorists have failed to describe adequately the right in question and have therefore come into conflict with other theorists. In particular, I have tried to show that those who espouse a view of privacy as a negative form of freedom have failed utterly to understand the natural distinction between these two entities and their natural interdependence at every level within the ontological structure of natural rights. Those who wish to reduce our right to privacy to other trade rights have failed to see innate privacy and autonomy, with their metaphorical representation in human dignity, as the very source of the rights to which they reduce our privacy rights. Even those who have wanted to espouse a view of privacy as a natural right have generally espoused only a weak view; they argue that privacy is grounded in human dignity but then assume either that human dignity is an elusive, factually innate human property or that grounding a right in "human dignity" does not require any explanation of human dignity.

Finally, I hope that my view has clarified the weakness of natural rights theories that see obligation to individuals as given in birth: in failing to see the requirement that natural rights be nevertheless culturally bestowed, these theories ignore both the significance of cultural differences in what rights are bestowed (both specifically and in terms of whether they emphasize the private or autonomous aspects of dignity) and the disputes that occur within Western culture over entitlement. By the same token, those who see such rights as the right to privacy as conventionally created and bestowed fail to account adequately for individual claims that fly in the face of convention or for the tenacity with which claims are staked. I have outlined the usefulness of what I propose not only for understanding our rights but also for understanding where other theories have gone wrong. The capacity of the theory to achieve both these ends is, I hope, part of its philosophical strength, which I have attempted to enhance by including the findings of other disciplines within the arguments.

It should be abundantly clear why I began by rejecting the possibility of defining our right to privacy; no verbal capsule could express the complexity of this natural right. To define our right to privacy as the right "to be let alone" is to define it by its most superficial metaphorical manifestation as the fluctuating right to a private life. In this case, it is conceived as a negative right. To define it as the right to information control is to define it positively but still superficially as the control aspect of its trade bestowal. Both of these common definitions portray our right to privacy as it appears to be within the trade. Neither recognizes the depth of its source in nature or of its contribution to the universal psychological construction of human dignity. Rendering the complexity of our right to privacy has required the rejection of verbal definitions in favour of a complex verbal picture of the ontological structure of this right, and of natural rights in general. It has required that a new ontological category of the moral be established as functioning within the factual ontology of our birth in order, metaphorically, to bring meaning to that birth. It has required no less than engaging the source of meaning in human existence and the function of the human capacity for metaphor to express that meaning to ourselves and to each other.

# Notes

INTRODUCTION

1 Though there are many such views, I focus on that of Clark, "Privacy, Property." Clark's article is particularly useful because it is written in response to the work of Wasserstrom ("Arguments and Assumptions"), who argues that privacy is distinct and rooted in human dignity.

2 Again, there are many who hold this view. I shall focus on Prosser ("Legal Analysis") and Thomson ("The Right to Privacy").

3 While I have already mentioned Wasserstrom as an advocate of this view, I focus also on Bloustein ("Privacy as an Aspect of Human Dignity"). Bloustein makes one of the most comprehensive attempts to unpack human dignity as that which is at stake in privacy claims. He does not, however, provide an adequate account of their connection.

4 See Schoeman, *Social Freedom*.

5 See Melden, *Rights and Persons*. Though Melden's work is on natural rights rather than privacy specifically, I refer to it in defending my own theory of natural rights, from which my theory of privacy can be extracted.

6 The concept of the "sacred self," which is now commonly used to refer to the core aspect of personhood that is protected through privacy claims, originated with Warren and Brandeis's conception of "inviolate personality" in "The Right to Privacy."

7 Hillel Steiner refers to natural rights as "non-created" or "original"; see *Essay on Rights*, 228–9.
8 *Oxford English Dictionary*, 2d ed., s.v. "rite."
9 Ibid., s.v. "sacred."
10 Wheelwright, *Fountain*, 97.
11 MacDonald, "Natural Rights," 24.
12 Ibid., 27.

CHAPTER ONE

1 Warren and Brandeis, "The Right to Privacy," 75.
2 Feinberg, "Nature and Value of Rights," 198.
3 Ibid., 197.
4 Ibid., 198.
5 I wish to emphasize that in referring to "natural properties," I refer to natural rights at any point in the ontology of natural rights before which they are "validated," as eliciting obligations, or duties, of others. By the same token, "natural rights" are natural properties as they appear at any point in the ontology of natural rights after which obligation has been bestowed upon the bearers of those properties.
6 To understand the difference I conceive between "psychological self-identity" and "philosophical personal identity," it is useful to bear in mind Mary Schectman's distinction between the "characterization question" of personal identity and the "re-identification question" of personal identity. The latter she identifies as the philosophical question "What makes a person at time $t_2$ the same person as at time $t_1$"; this question would apply to my conception of *personal* identity. The former she identifies as the question which "beliefs, values, desires, and other psychological features make someone the person she is." At least insofar as the characterization question requires self-knowledge and analysis, it is related to my conception of *self*-identity. See Schectman, *Constitution*, 1–2.
7 Briere and Runtz, "Long-Term Effects," 7.
8 Westerlund, *Women's Sexuality*, 46.
9 See note 7.
10 Thought-violation machines appear throughout ethical, and even epistemological, discourse. With reference to privacy, specifically, Richard A. Wasserstrom asks us to suppose "existing technology made it possible for an outsider in some way to look into or monitor another's mind. What … would be especially disturbing about that?" See Wasserstrom, "Arguments and Assumptions," 153.

11 An interesting discussion that is relevant to my discussion can be found in Kamm, *Morality, Mortality*, 279–80. After arguing that certain constraints follow from a conception of the person as inviolable, Kamm asks whether that conception is true, whether it is just an attractive picture, or whether it is one we are better off believing. Though she does not herself argue for any particular view, she does offer both the possibility of the view I defend, of the truly, though minimally, inviolable person, and the possibility of what I shall argue in chapter 3, of legitimately deriving rights from a conception of personhood.

12 An important discussion of the link between human dignity and self-control can be found in Meyer, "Dignity, Rights, and Self-Control." The connection between human rights and human dignity" is not as significant as the connection between human dignity and self-control. Indeed, at page 533, he tells us not only that to *express* dignity must one have some self-control but also that "the capacity to exercise self-control is necessary if one is to be said to *have* dignity," (my emphasis). Meyer recognizes both that dignity can be diminished through lack of self-control and that it cannot be *fully* lost, in the sense that someone's failure at self-control "does not provide others with the privilege to treat him like an object or deprive him of the status of a human being" (ibid., 9). He does not, however, examine either the human properties at the base of the link between self-control and dignity, or the reason *why* one person's loss of self-control is not another's license to transgress his dignity. On my model, thus far, dignity cannot be fully lost only in the sense that the properties that cause us to conceive of ourselves as dignified cannot be fully violated. Later it will become evident that the conception of humans as dignified is a moral ideal, adopted universally, which must not be transgressed because it both represents essential human properties and grounds all valid claims regarding those properties.

It is difficult to tell whether Meyer sees human dignity as innate or as a status *earned* through self-control. If indeed he holds that the privilege denied us to treat as an object any individual flagrantly lacking self-control is denied on the basis of what is required to maintain our *own* dignity (self-control), then it is possible to think that he does not hold human dignity to be innate. At any rate, I do not hold it to be so, though it bears a complex relationship to properties and modes of self-conception that are innate. The question what it is about dignity that links it to self-control (its origins in human nature) I shall now address in the body of the text.

13 *Oxford English Dictionary*, 2d ed., s.v. "dignity."

14 In illuminating the centrality of self-control, rather than rights, to human dignity, Meyer emphasizes that self-control may require the shy man to "control [his] apprehensions long enough to claim [his] rights" or a black man to restrain his anger when "faced with the abusive town idiot." See Meyer, "Dignity," 8. I say that Meyer's "shy man" overcomes his shyness to exercise autonomy and maintain the dignity of agency, while Meyer's "black man" exercises his privacy through concealing his anger to maintain dignity in the face of one who has none.

Some might wonder, at this point, whether the fact that our internal organs are not on view puts them at the core of our concern for privacy. The ontology of concealment, however, cannot really be seen to apply to the concealment of internal organs because the sense in which thoughts might be "on view" is not that of seeing them or even of observing their function. Rather, it is in the sense of accessing/controlling their content or meaning. Moreover, even if we could conceive of internal organs as part of the initial ontology of concealment, we cannot conceive of them as part of the whole picture, which includes the construction of dignity/rights on the basis of our innately concealed (and agential) natures. Our internal organs are not something we either perceive or conceive of as private in the way a thing must be private to be essential to personhood. Thoughts, and therefore the processes that make them, can be and are conceived of in this way.

15 It is important that I here briefly address psychological literature in support of the essentialist claims I make about people. There seem to be two pertinent schools of thought regarding the ontological status of human dignity (as either "innate" or a function of self-conceiving). These can be broadly labelled the "humanist" and the "behaviourist" schools and shall be represented here by the views of Moser, in *The Struggle for Human Dignity*, and Skinner, in *Beyond Freedom and Dignity*.

From the outset, it is important to note that both Moser (the "humanist") and Skinner link freedom (or autonomy) with the conception of human dignity, and that Moser discusses privacy or "seclusion" as also necessary to dignity and identity, saying that "man must experience himself in isolation before he can grasp the deepest meaning of his existence" and that "only through [this isolation] … can a person maintain a truthful self-identity" (Moser, *Struggle*, 124).

That autonomy and privacy are linked to human dignity, then, is unquestioned in the literature.

Moser takes exception, however, to what she sees as Skinner's rejection of the dignity of "man," saying that in viewing dignity as the "amount of credit a man receives from his fellows" Skinner claims that dignity "is ascribed to man by man, and is not at all intrinsic" (ibid., 27). She prefers Lawrence Kohlberg's work on the "universal values of human life" (ibid.), which has shown that "moral development proceeds from a cognitive core," and in which "the universality of moral judgment reflecting human dignity and the value of life are well-demonstrated" (ibid., 24, speaking about Kohlberg, "The Development of Moral Character"). Indeed, the implications of Skinner's claims regarding the ascription of dignity to people have been broadly criticized even to the point where Skinner finally claimed to have been "misunderstood." See Skinner, *Beyond Freedom*.

While the present theory of natural rights does claim that we are not inherently dignified, let me not be misunderstood. There is no reason to suppose that because we have an innate tendency to view ourselves morally as dignified (Kohlberg's view), we are therefore innately dignified, and certainly not in the way that we are innately private and autonomous. For thought itself is innately (or, at least, has an innate capacity to be) free and private, though it is not innately dignified. In speaking of the priority of privacy and autonomy I speak at least of their factual existence as properties of people's thoughts. It is only through self-perception and definition that we can come to a conception of people as dignified. Such a view is not contrary to a Kohlbergian view of universal moral development (indeed, my theory relies on such a view), but neither is it committed to a claim of innate dignity for humans.

16 Such a theory can be found in Hixson, *Privacy in a Public Society*. Yet even where "community" is not solidly enough entrenched to provide the systematic bestowal of rights (such as within the international community), claims are staked.

17 Evidence of the universality of claims regarding both physical and psychological natural properties can be found not only in anthropological studies, to be cited presently, but also in psychological studies such as Kohlberg's, where we learn that "every culture [he has studied] … has used the same moral norms and elements in the same structural developmental sequence, a sequence that has the property of increasing universalizability" (Kohlberg, *Essays*, 2:283). Most

significant to the present discussion is Kohlberg's observation of the universality of "the development of structures of justice reasoning" (ibid., 287) in conjunction with his observation that among the "moral norms and elements that have been used by moral reasoners in all the cultures" is the "ideal or harmony-serving" norm of serving "human dignity and autonomy" (ibid., 287, 309). He argues, then, that humans *all* have the capacity both to conceive of the self (and then others) as dignified and to "serve," or act upon, duty to human dignity. This we do through developing privacy, autonomy, and other dignity norms. The universality of the claims I here identify is born of the universality of human moral development, or ways of self-conceiving.

18 In spite of Carol Gilligan's objection to the "justice" framework of Kohlberg's theory, which, she argues, excludes "care" as a significant moral concept, *her* work supports another aspect of my view of natural rights. She herself initiated the notion that "conceptions of self and morality might be intricately linked" and that "modes of moral judgment might be related to modes of self-definitions." See Lyons, "Two Perspectives," 23. At the basis of my model of natural rights is a drawing together of the Kohlbergian universal acceptance of the ideal of human dignity with a Gilliganesque notion that that universal ideal represents a way we have of defining/conceiving of ourselves. Gilligan may protest that not all people conceive of themselves as inherently dignified, but even she would have to admit that the failure so to conceive of oneself is a function of environmental or personal influences that are somehow unjust, perhaps even abnormal.

19 The link between dignity and rights can be found in varied sources. Already noted in the psychological literature (Moser, *Struggle*, Skinner, *Beyond Freedom*, and Kohlberg, *Essays*, vol. 2), it is defended also by natural rights theorists such as Melden (*Rights and Persons*) and, with specific reference to privacy and autonomy rights, Bloustein ("Answer to Dean Prosser") and Wasserstrom ("Arguments and Assumptions"). Bloustein makes a comprehensive attempt to unpack human dignity as that which is at stake in privacy claims but does not provide an adequate account of the connection.

20 Wasserstrom ("Arguments and Assumptions") holds this view. Also, in their seminal article on privacy as a right ("The Right to Privacy"), Warren and Brandeis defend a conception of "inviolate personality" that is clearly linked to human dignity and is clearly innate.

21 Melden (*Rights and Persons*) holds this view.

22 The sample radical metaphor used by Max Muller is the Sanskrit root
term *arka*, meaning "to shine," which apparently forms part of the
names of many things from the sun itself, to a keen intellect, to a
"joyous outburst of hymns of praise." See Muller, *The Science of
Language*, 451.

23 Ibid.

24 Ibid.

25 Note that this question differs from the initial query of this section –
Why should society take measures to protect *inviolable*, absolute, natural rights? – in that the initial question *assumes* the moral significance
of innate privacy and autonomy. I now seek to clarify why such
significance is granted psychological natural properties.

26 Evidence of this can be found in Murphy ("Social Distance and the
Veil") and in Westin (*Privacy and Freedom*), among others.

27 This rather Hobbesian view of liberty, at the manifest symbolic level,
as being merely the right to walk about town, as it were, without
"external impediments of motion" might seem replaceable at first by
the broader "free speech" norms of Western culture. Free speech is,
after all, clearly a manifestation of free thought. Free speech norms,
however, are not static in the way that would allow us to view them
as cultural symbols. My right, in innocence, to walk to my car better
represents the *kind* of right I have to think freely than does this culture's very general, even idealistic, adherence to a right to free speech.
For the Hobbes reference, see Hobbes, *Leviathan*, 145.

28 In *Privacy and Freedom*, Westin refers to the practice among Eskimos
and certain Australian tribes of viewing an individual's name as
inherently private. Other cultures see eating as an inherently private
activity. Kohlberg points out that while "moral behaviors or customs
seem to vary from culture to culture, underneath these variations
in custom there seem to be universal kinds of judging or valuing."
See *Essays*, 2:283. To illustrate his point he observes that "culturally
variable customs of monogamy and polygamy are both compatible
with the culturally universal underlying moral norms of personal
dignity, commitment, and trust in sexual relationships"(ibid.).

CHAPTER TWO

1 While it is possible to choose not to exercise a right, for instance, to
walk to one's car, such a choice cannot properly be conceived as a
choice to "waive" that right. Moreover, even when incarceration for

illict behaviour precludes a right to walk *to one's car*, specifically, a right to walk about (within one's stipulated confines) remains, as long as one's motive for walking is innocent.

2 While it is possible to conceive that we might waive the right to privacy for defecation within the context of certain intimate relationships, the reality of the distinction between defecation and childbirth at the moral-symbolic level can be illustrated by first imagining a documentary film about childbirth, in which it is perfectly conceivable that an actual birthing might be shown. If we follow this by imagining a documentary about biological processes, we are alarmed to think of the possibility that someone might provide a demonstration of defecation. The act of sexual intercourse is also "taboo" when it comes to videographic demonstration, though much else to do with sexuality is not.

3 Schoeman, *Privacy and Social Freedom*, 7–8.

4 Ibid., 8–9.

5 Ibid., 16.

6 Ibid.

7 Ibid.

8 Ibid.

9 Ibid., 17.

10 Ibid., 15.

11 See Benn,"Privacy, Freedom, and Respect for Persons."

12 Schoeman, *Privacy and Social Freedom*, 17.

13 Ibid., 15.

14 In current parenting literature it is commonly advised that we teach small children to be proud of bodily functions that must nevertheless take place "in private." It is not the bodily function that is shameful but disregard for the inherent privacy of persons. Penelope Leach tells us that a toddler, for instance, "has just discovered that [faeces] … come out of him" and that if "he knows his feces are disgusting to you, he will feel that you think he is disgusting too." Leach, *Your Baby and Child*, 317.

15 Shoeman, *Privacy and Social Freedom*, 18.

16 Ibid., 18.

17 Clark, "Privacy, Property …", 168. Other proponents of the view that privacy as a right is reducible to a form of freedom as a right include Gross ("Privacy and Autonomy"). At page 181, Gross tells us that "while an offense to privacy is an offense to autonomy, not every curtailment of autonomy is a compromise of privacy."

18 Ibid., 168.

19 See Wasserstrom, "Arguments and Assumptions."

20 Ibid., 154, and Clark, "Privacy, Property," 175.

21 Clark, "Privacy, Property," 175.

22 Ibid., 176.

23 Ibid.

24 Wasserstrom, "Arguments and Assumptions," 154.

25 Another such theorist is Edward Bloustein. In "Answer to Dean Prosser" he addresses Prosser's reductionism by saying that all privacy claims are claims in defence of human dignity. Like Wasserstrom, however, he fails to provide adequate analysis of the concept of human dignity.

26 Clark, "Privacy, Property," 175. Clark discusses the issue of monitoring thoughts when she tells us that "metaphysical realities are irrelevant to the moral issues. If the moral and/or legal guidelines are laid down, then the metaphysical outcomes do not matter." She fails to recognize that creating and evaluating moral or legal guidelines inevitably takes people back to questions of nature and metaphysics at some point.

27 Ibid., 186.

28 Ernst and Schwartz, *Right to be Let Alone*, 12.

29 See Westin, *Privacy and Freedom*.

30 Ibid., 34.

31 Ibid., 322.

32 Neither do we yet fully violate privacy, for as long as we autonomously produce our own thoughts the "who it is" that produces the thought is not known. Through autonomy we maintain the privacy of personal identity.

33 See Simmel, "Privacy Is Not an Isolated Freedom."

34 See Freund, "Privacy: One Concept or Many."

35 Simmel, "Privacy Is Not an Isolated Freedom," 72.

36 See Murphy, "Social Distance and the Veil," and Westin, *Privacy and Freedom*.

37 Simmel, "Privacy Is Not an Isolated Freedom," 72.

38 Freund, "Privacy: One Concept or Many," 182.

39 Ibid., 192.

40 Ibid.

41 Ibid., 193.

42 Ibid., 194.

43 Ibid.

44 Ibid., 196.
45 Ibid., 197.

CHAPTER THREE

1 Moore, *Principia*. Moore invented the term "naturalistic fallacy."
2 Fried, "Analysis," 475–93.
3 Ibid., 214.
4 Schoeman also provides support for viewing certain privacy norms as symbolic. Moreover, he distinguishes *two* types of privacy norms that correspond quite well to my static and fluctuating norms. These I shall discuss in the fifth chapter in the context of exploring what it is to transgress privacy. Suffice it for now to say that Schoeman, like Fried, sees these symbols as reflective of social rather than innate individual necessity. See Schoeman, *Privacy and Social Freedom*.
5 This I argued in chapter 1 on grounds of their mutual attachment to conceptions of self-control referring to Meyer, "Dignity."
6 Hume's attack on ethical naturalism appears in both the *Treatise* and the *Enquiry*.
7 I am indebted to Samantha Brennan both for raising this problem and for this formulation of it.
8 There are two dominant theories of metaphor in the literature. That I subscribe to the "romantic theory" is evidenced by the fact that I believe metaphor *adds* meaning, rather than just conveys it, and is part of what we use to *create* reality. This theory originated with Plato (implicitly) and was elaborated both by Neoplatonists and by the Romantic poets, such as Wordsworth, Shelley, and Coleridge. It finds modern expression in the works, for example, of Max Black, Philip Wheelwright, and I.A. Richards's "interaction theory" of metaphor. In his description of Richards's theory, Terence Hawkes tells us that, in his view, language is not "the medium through which we communicate to each other information about a reality that already exists in the 'real world' outside us. On the contrary, language *causes* that reality to exist … Metaphor intensifies language's characteristic activity, and involves, quite literally, the creation of a 'new' reality" (Hawkes, *Metaphor*, 58). I view "reality" as being some combination of objective and constructed facts.

  The other "classical," or "literal meaning," theory of metaphor involves the view that metaphors are falsehoods that yet convey some meaning. This view originated with Aristotle, Cicero, and Longinus and finds modern expression, both explicitly and implicitly, in the works of such thinkers as Grice, Searle, Davidson, and Rorty. The view assumes that metaphor is somehow " 'detachable' from language; a device that may be imparted into language to achieve specific … effects. These aid language to achieve what is seen as its major goal, the revelation of the 'reality' of a world that lies, unchanging, beyond it" (ibid., 90). In this view, to see moral qualities like human dignity as metaphorical is to see them as falsehoods capable of communicating, but not generating, meaning and reality. My argument speaks of value's being literally "added to" facts, through metaphor, rather than being deduced from them. Metaphor's ability to do this is the source of the "dual ontology" of my theory in which moral qualities, and conclusions, *are* metaphorically constructed but are not therefore "false" and do not bear less "reality" than the properties that are foundational to their construction.

9 Haakonssen, "Grotius," 239–65.
10 Ibid., 252.
11 Ibid., 240.
12 Ibid., 252.
13 Ibid.
14 Ibid., 887.
15 Ibid.
16 Ibid., 240.
17 Ibid.
18 Ibid.
19 Ibid., 242.
20 Ibid., 252.
21 Melden, *Rights and Persons*.
22 Ibid., 2.
23 Ibid.
24 Ibid., 166.
25 Ibid., 185.
26 Ibid., 192.
27 Ibid., 199.
28 Ibid., 195.
29 Ibid., 194.
30 Kohlberg, *Essays*, vols. 1 and 2.
31 Kohlberg, *Essays* 2:xv.
32 Ibid.
33 Ibid., 173.

34 Ibid.

35 Ibid.

36 Ibid., 178.

37 Ibid.

38 Ibid., 318.

39 Ibid., 636.

40 Ibid., 318.

41 Ibid., 637.

42 Ibid., 266.

43 Ibid., 284.

44 Ibid. (my emphasis).

45 Ibid. 285 (my emphasis).

46 Ibid. 285 (my emphasis).

47 Ibid., 283.

48 Ibid.

49 Turiel, *Moral Development*, quoted in Kohlberg, *Essays* 2:283–4.

50 Kohlberg, *Essays* 2:284.

51 Ibid.

52 Indeed, Kohlberg himself posits a seventh "high soft stage in the development of ethical and religious orientations," which I shall discuss in more detail when I come to situate my theory both within and outside Kohlberg's. See Kohlberg, *Essays* 2:249.

53 Ibid., 285.

54 Ibid., 286.

55 Ibid.

56 Kanjirathinkal, *Critique*.

57 Ibid., 90.

58 Ibid.

59 Edwards, "Consensus," 427.

60 Kanjirathinkal, Critique, 60.

61 Edwards, "Consensus," 451.

62 In his critical response to Edwards's support of Kohlberg, Ian Vine admits that "recent research findings are broadly compatible with the universality postulate." See Vine, "Moral Maturity," 436.

63 Kohlberg, *Essays* 2:286.

64 Ibid., 286–7.

65 Ibid., xv.

66 Ibid., 287.

67 Ibid.

68 Ibid.

69 Kohlberg, *Essays* 1:177.
70 Ibid., 177–8.
71 Ibid., 181.
72 Ibid.
73 Ibid.
74 Ibid., 178.
75 Ibid.
76 Ibid.
77 Ibid., 180.
78 Kohlberg, *Essays* 2:249.
79 Ibid., 249–50.
80 Ibid., 250.
81 Ibid.

CHAPTER FOUR

1 See Prosser, "Legal Analysis."
2 See Thomson, "Right to Privacy."
3 See Schoeman, *Social Freedom.*
4 See Melden, *Rights and Persons.*
5 Prosser, "Legal Analysis," 107.
6 Ibid., 124.
7 Thomson, "Right to Privacy," 287.
8 Prosser, "Legal Analysis," 107.
9 Thomson, "Right to Privacy," 287.
10 Ibid., 286.
11 Among those who have attempted to analyze the notion of human dignity as what is at the core in privacy claims is Bloustein, in "Privacy as an aspect of Human Dignity." While Bloustein shows that each of the "interests" to which Prosser reduces privacy claims has human dignity as *its* core, and while he argues also that moral personality would be lost by anyone subject completely to public scrutiny, he does not adequately describe human dignity. He assumes it to be a factually innate human feature and therefore leaves his argument open to the charge of an essentialism that is much further reaching than that upon which my argument relies. He leaves open the question whether we are *factually* innately dignified and so leaves all established rights open to collapse in the event that we are not, which we are not. Dignity, with morality itself, is a construction.
12 Prosser, "Legal Analysis," 125.

13 Scanlon, "Thomson on Privacy."

14 Ibid., 317.

15 Ibid., 317–18.

16 Ibid., 318.

17 Ibid.

18 Ibid., 319.

19 Thomson, "Right to Privacy," 287.

20 Schoeman, *Social Freedom*, 115–35.

21 Ibid., 115.

22 Ibid.

23 Ibid., 135.

24 Ibid., 116.

25 Ibid., 117.

26 Ibid., 125.

27 A discussion of this fact, along with the examples used by Schoeman, can be found in Aries and Duby, *Private Life*.

28 See Aries and Duby, *Private Life*, 161–81.

29 In *Essays*, vol. 1, Kohlberg outlines his theory of cultural evolutionism. Based on studies he and others conducted, Kohlberg finds that "moral stage development tends to be assessed at lower stages in less developed, village cultures, whereas in highly developed, urban societies moral development proceeds to the highest stages, at least in some individuals." See p. 234. On the basis of these findings he holds that Stage Six moral principles "would in fact be universal to all humankind if the conditions for sociomoral development were optimal for all individuals in all cultures." See p. 28.

30 Aries and Duby, *Private Life*, 30–1.

31 Ibid., 31.

32 Schoeman, *Social Freedom*, 115.

33 See Elias, *The Civilizing Process*. Schoeman introduces him in *Social Freedom*, 118.

34 See Stone, *Family, Sex and Marriage*. Schoeman introduces him in *Social Freedom*, 123.

35 See Flaherty, *Colonial New England*. Schoeman refers to him for the present purposes in *Social Freedom*, 125.

36 See Trilling, *Sincerity & Authenticity*. Schoeman introduces him in *Social Freedom*, 131.

37 Schoeman, *Social Freedom*, 118.

38 Ibid., 119.

39 Ibid., 122–3.
40 Ibid., 125.
41 Ibid., 127.
42 Ibid., 135.

CHAPTER FIVE

1 The reader will remember what was established in the first chapter, that though innate privacy and autonomy are ultimately non-transgressible (inviolable), static norms are put in place not only to provide concrete access to the transgression of human dignity but, in doing so, to represent the societal decision to revere and symbolically protect innate properties. Our duty to the concept of dignity implies a norm against *attempting* to violate what cannot be fully violated.

2 This is not, of course, all that makes them natural. The universality of dignity and its constituent properties as values that ground rights is also fundamentally linked to the claim of innateness for the rights constructed.

3 See Flaherty 1996.

4 Ibid., 75.

5 Ibid., 81.

6 Ibid.

7 Ibid., 78.

8 A 1997 Supreme Court of Canada decision eliminated the absolute right of privacy for psychiatrist/patient relationships. In *M.(A.)* v. *Ryan* (1997) 143 D.L.R. (4th) 1, Justice McLachlin (with LaForest, Sopinka, Cory, Iacobucci, and Major JJ. concurring) found that the privilege shielding private psychiatric records from disclosure was a "partial privilege." In her dissent, Justice L'Heureux-Dubé quoted McNaughton (1961) in referring to this privilege as a "case-by-case" privilege, in which "the communications are not privileged *unless the party opposing disclosure can show that they should be privileged ...*" (*Supra* at 18). She quotes McNaughton as comparing this case-by-case privilege to a "class privilege" which entails a "presumption that such communications are inadmissible or not subject to disclosure *in criminal or civil proceedings and the onus lies on the party seeking disclosure of the information to show that an overriding interest commands disclosure ...*" (*Supra* at 18). While L'Heureux-Dubé agrees that the public interest in "correctly disposing of legal disputes" can outweigh

its interest in "fostering particular relationships" (*Supra* at 21), i.e., the particular confidentiality of therapist/patient relationships, she feels that in allowing psychiatric records to be handed over to defendants without previous screening, by the Court, for relevance, the Supreme Court of Canada admits a hierarchy of Charter values, "where interests in privacy and equality may be seriously affected for records which may provide ... little if any benefit to the defence or be unnecessary to ensure the fairness of the proceedings" (*Supra* at 37).
She argues, then, that privacy, which *is* a Charter interest, has not been granted its due status *as a social ideal* in the decision of the Court.

More recently, in *R. v. Mills*, the Supreme Court has allowed an appeal in which the Crown is seeking to protect the privacy of a victim whose counselling records have been deemed, by a lower court, "fair game" for the defence to employ in making full answer and defence. The appeal has been allowed on grounds that the competing rights of privacy and full answer must be weighed on a case-by-case basis within the context of the circumstances and principles involved. In this case, the importance of privacy for counselling records is linked to the importance of respecting mental integrity and security of the person. See *R. v. Mills (1999)* [Quicklaw].

9 Max Rosenbaum tells us that confidentiality "protects the client or patient ... Many therapists believe that confidentiality should be absolute and that *no* circumstances justify the breach of confidentiality." See Rosenbaum 1982, 251. Confidentiality is essential to treatment because "all censorship of items of thought must be removed and whatever emerges should be declared without regard to shame or to offending the therapist." See Sim 1974, 904.

10 See Fried 1984. At page 209–10, Fried argues against the "desert island" scenario in which a lonely man is seen to have privacy for being alone. He stipulates that to "refer ... to the privacy of [such a man] ... would be to engage in irony. The person who enjoys privacy is able to grant or deny access to others ... Privacy, thus, is control over [both] the quantity ... [and] the quality of ... knowledge ... [about oneself]."

While I agree with Fried that control is an essential element of privacy, I believe that what we need to control is the perception of ourselves as dignified, whether it is our own perception or that of a potential observer. This perception can be maintained through the most basic of static norms without entailing our hiding underground to remain unobserved. Human symbolic expression is much more powerful than many theorists allow.

11 See *R. v. Pietrangelo* (1999) [Quicklaw]. In this case, Mr Pietrangelo was alleged to have been snorting cocaine in a washroom stall when police entered the stall and did indeed find cocaine on his person. The judge determined that Mr Pietrangelo's Charter right to privacy had been violated because the police officer had no warrant and did not know whether or not the accused was engaged in "embarrassing" activity before the officer entered the stall.

CONCLUSION

1 See *R. v. Jacob* (1997) 31 O.R. (3d) 350.

# Bibliography

Arendt, Hannah. *The Human Condition*. Chicago: University of Chicago Press, 1958.

Aries, Philippe, and Georges Duby. eds. *A History of Private Life*. Vol. 1: *From Pagan Rome to Byzantium*. Cambridge: Harvard University Press, 1987.

Becker, Lawrence, ed. *Encyclopedia of Ethics*. London: Garland Publishing, 1992.

Benn, Stanley. "Privacy, Freedom, and Respect for Persons." In *Philosophical Dimensions of Privacy*, edited by Ferdinand Schoeman. Cambridge: Cambridge University Press, 1984.

Bloustein, Edward. "Privacy as an Aspect of Human Dignity: An Answer to Dean Prosser." In *Philosophical Dimensions of Privacy*, edited by Ferdinand Schoeman. Cambridge: Cambridge University Press, 1984.

Briere, John, ed. *Treating Victims of Child Abuse*. San Francisco: Jossey Bass, 1992.

Briere, John, and Marsha Runtz. "The Long-Term Effects of Sexual Abuse." In *Treating Victims of Child Abuse*, edited by John Briere. San Francisco: Jossey Bass, 1992.

Bronaugh, Richard, ed. *Philosophical Law*. Westport: Greenwood Press, 1978.

Clark, Lorenne M.G. "Privacy, Property, Freedom, and the Family." In Philosophical Law, edited by Richard Bronaugh. Westport: Greenwood Press, 1978.

Edwards, Carolyn Pope. "Cross-Cultural Research on Kohlberg's Stages: The Basis for Consensus." In *Lawrence Kohlberg: Consensus and Controversy*, edited by Sohan Mogdil and Celia Mogdil, 419–30, 451. Philadelphia: Falmer Press, 1985.

Elias, Norbert. *The Civilizing Process*. Vol. I: *History of Manners*. New York: Urizen Books, 1978. Vol. 2: *Power and Civility*. New York: Pantheon Books, 1982.

Ernst, Morris L., and Alan U. Schwartz. *Privacy: The Right to be Let Alone*. London: Macmillan, 1962.

Feinberg, Joel. "The Nature and Value of Rights." In *Rights*, edited by Carlos Nino. New York: New York University Press, 1992.

Flaherty, David. "Privacy, Confidentiality, and the Use of Canadian Health Information for Research and Statistics." *Canadian Public Administration* 35, no. 1 (1996): 75–93.

Flaherty, David. Privacy in Colonial New England. Charlottesville: University of Virginia Press, 1972.

Frankena, W.K. "The Naturalistic Fallacy." *Mind* 10, no. 58. London: Macmillan, 1939.

Freedman, Warren. *The Right of Privacy in the Computer Age*. New York: Quorum Books, 1987.

Freund, Paul A. "Privacy: One Concept or Many." In *Nomos 18: Privacy*, edited by J. Roland Pennock and John W. Chapman. New York: Atherton Press, 1971.

Fried, Charles. "Privacy: A Moral Analysis." In *Philosophical Dimensions of Privacy*, edited by Ferdinand Silverman. Cambridge: Cambridge University Press, 1984.

Gilligan, Carol, Janie Victoria Ward, and Jill McLean Taylor, eds. *Mapping the Moral Domain*. Cambridge: Harvard University Press, 1988.

Gross, Hyman. "Privacy and Autonomy." In *Nomos 18: Privacy*, edited by J. Roland Pennock and John W. Chapman. New York: Atherton Press, 1971.

Haakonssen, Knud. "Hugo Grotius and the History of Political Thought." *Political Theory* 15 (1985): 239–65.

Haakonssen, Knud. "Natural Law." in *Encyclopedia of Ethics*, edited by Laurence Becker. London: Garland Publishing, 1992.

Hawkes, Terrence. *Metaphor*. London: Methuen, 1972.

Hixson, Richard F. *Privacy in a Public Society*. Oxford: Oxford University Press, 1987.

Hobbes, Thomas. *Leviathan*. Edited by Richard Tuck. Cambridge: Cambridge University Press, 1992.

Hoffman, M., ed. *Review of Child Psychology*. New York: Russell Sage Foundation, 1964.

Hume, David. *An Enquiry Concerning the Principles of Morals*. Edited by Lewis Amherst Selby-Bigge. Oxford: Clarendon Press, 1995.

– *A Treatise on Human Nature*. Edited by Lewis Amherst Selby-Bigge. Oxford: Clarendon Press, 1985.

Kamm, Frances. *Morality, Mortality*. Vol. 2. Oxford: Oxford University Press, 1996.

Kanjirathinkal, Matthew J. *A Sociological Critique of Theories of Cognitive Development: The Limitations of Piaget and Kohlberg*. Lewiston: Edward Mellen Press, 1990.

Kohlberg, Lawrence. "The Development of Moral Character and Ideology." In *Review of Child Psychology*, edited by M. Hoffman. New York: Russell Sage Foundation, 1964.

– *Essays on Moral Development*. Vol. 1, *The Philosophy of Moral Development*. San Francisco: Harper and Row, 1981. Vol. 2, *The Psychology of Moral Development*. San Francisco: Harper and Row, 1984.

– *The Psychology of Moral Development: The Nature and Validity of Moral Stages*. San Francisco: Harper and Row, 1984.

Leach, Penelope. *Your Baby and Child: From Birth to Age Five*. New York: Alfred A. Knopf, 1994.

Lyons, Nona P. "Two Perspectives: On Self, Relationship, and Morality." In *Mapping the Moral Domain*, edited by Carol Gilligan et al. Cambridge: Haward University Press, 1988.

*M.A. v. Ryan* (1997) 143 D.L.R. (4th) 1.

Macdonald, Margaret. "Natural Rights." In *Theories of Rights*, edited by Jeremy Waldron. Oxford: Oxford University Press, 1984.

Melden, Abraham Irving. *Rights and Persons*. Berkeley: University of California Press, 1977.

Meyer, Michael J. "Dignity, Rights, and Self-Control." *Ethics* 99 (1989): 520–34.

Mogdil, Sohan, and Mogdil, Celia. eds. *Lawrence Kohlberg: Consensus and Controversy*. Philadelphia: Falmer Press, 1985.

Moore, G.E. *Principia Ethica*. Cambridge: Cambridge University Press, 1903.

Moser, Leslie E. *The Struggle for Human Dignity*. Los Angeles: Nash Publishing, 1973.

Muller, Frederick. *The Science of Language*. London: Longmans, Green, 1899.

Murphy, Robert. "Social Distance and the Veil." *American Anthropologist* 66, no. 6, pt. 1 (1964): 34–55.

Nino, Carlos, ed. *Rights.* New York: New York University Press, 1992.

Pennock, J. Roland, and John W. Chapman. eds. *Nomos 18: Privacy.* New York: Atherton Press, 1971.

Prosser, William, L. "Privacy [A Legal Analysis]." In *Philosophical Dimensions of Privacy,* edited by Fardinand Schoeman Cambridge: Cambridge University Press, 1984.

*R. v. Jacob.* 31 *Ontario Reports* 3rd. Toronto: Butterworths, 1997.

*R. v. Mills. Quicklaw,* 1999.

*R. v. Pietrangelo. Quicklaw,* 1999.

Rosenbaum, Max, ed. *Ethics and Values in Psychotherapy.* New York: Free Press, 1982.

Rosenbaum, Max. "Ethical Problems of Group Psychotherapy." in Rosenbaum. *Ethics and Values in Psychotherapy,* edited by Max Rosenbaum. New York: Free Press, 1982.

Schectman, Marya. *The Constitution of Selves.* Ithaca: Cornell University Press, 1996.

Schoeman, Ferdinand. *Privacy and Social Freedom.* Cambridge: Cambridge University Press, 1992.

Schoeman, Ferdinand, ed. *Philosophical Dimensions of Privacy.* Cambridge: Cambridge University Press, 1984.

Sim, Myre. *Guide to Psychiatry.* London: Churchill Livingstone, 1974.

Simmel, Arnold. "Privacy Is Not an Isolated Freedom." in Pennock and Chapman. *Nomos 18: Privacy,* edited by J. Roland Pennock and John W. Chapman. New York: Atherton Press, 1971.

Skinner, Burrhus Frederic. *Beyond Freedom and Dignity.* New York: Alfred A. Knopf, 1971.

– "I Have Been Misunderstood …" *The Center Magazine* (1972).

Steiner, Hillel. *An Essay on Rights.* Oxford: Blackwell, 1994.

Stone, Lawrence. *The Family, Sex and Marriage in England, 1500–1800.* New York: Harper and Row, 1977.

Thomson, Judith Jarvis. "The Right to Privacy." In *Philosophical Dimensions of Privacy,* edited by Ferdinand Shoeman. Cambridge: Cambridge University Press, 1984.

Trilling, Lionel. *Sincerity and Authenticity.* Cambridge: Harvard University Press, 1972.

Turiel, Elliott. *Moral Development and Socialization,* edited by Myra Windmiller and Nadine Lambert, Elliott Turiel. Boston: Allyn and Bacon, 1980.

Vine, Ian. "Moral Maturity in Socio-Cultural Perspective: Are Kohlberg's Stages Universal?" In *Lawrence Kohlberg: Consensus and Controversy,* edited by Sohan Mogdil and Celia Mogdil, 431–50. Philadelphia: Falmer Press, 1985.

Waldron, Jeremy, ed. *Theories of Rights*. Oxford: Oxford University Press, 1984.

Warren, Samuel D., and Louis D. Brandeis. "The Right to Privacy [The Implicit Made Explicit]." In *Philosophical Dimensions of Privacy*, edited by Ferdinand Shoeman. Cambridge: Cambridge University Press, 1984.

Wasserstrom, Richard A. "Privacy: Some Arguments and Assumptions." In *Philosophical Law*, edited by Richard Bronaugh. Westport: Greenwood Press, 1978.

Westerlund, Elaine. *Women's Sexuality After Childhood Incest*. New York: W.W. Norton, 1992.

Westin, Alan. *Privacy and Freedom*. New York: Atheneum, 1968.

Wheelwright, Philip. *The Burning Fountain*. Bloomington: Indiana University Press, 1959.

# Index